The World as a Stage

EDITED BY JESSICA MORGAN & CATHERINE WOOD

TATE PUBLISHING

First published 2007 by order of the Tate Trustees
by Tate Publishing, a division of Tate Enterprises Ltd,
Millbank, London SW1P 4RG, www.tate.org.uk/publishing

On the occasion of the exhibition at Tate Modern, London
24 October 2007 – 1 January 2008
and touring to the Institute of Contemporary Art, Boston
1 February – 27 April 2008

A catalogue record for this book is available from the British Library

ISBN 978 1 85437 760 9

Distributed in the United States and Canada by
Harry N. Abrams, Inc., New York

Library of Congress Control Number: 2007934780

Publication designed by APFEL, London
Advertisements on pp.6, 12, 13 designed by APFEL, London
Artist's portraits on pp.16–19 by Paul Ryan, London
Printed in Spain by Grafos, Barcelona

CONTENT

FOREWORD

The World as a Stage presents a key group of international contemporary artists whose practices reinvigorate the rich historical relationship between visual art and theatre. Challenging the negative associations made between the notion of 'theatricality' and the realm of visual art in recent decades, the artists in this exhibition make visible the extent to which a sense of theatre now permeates one's role as a spectator in the gallery space and how this is carried through to an experience of the contemporary urban environment.

Works in the exhibition test the boundaries between the compact architectural design of the white cube gallery space and the wider public sphere, setting them in dialogue. The gallery, as a theatrically 'neutral' stage for individual contemplation, is positioned in relation to the self-reflexive awareness that it generates in the spectator's perception of the world at large. In a stimulating series of installations, video, film and event, the idea of 'theatre' is treated by the artists in *The World as a Stage* as both an analytic tool and a rich terrain to be explored, experimented with, and plundered.

We are enormously grateful to all the artists involved for their work in realising this exhibition. Pawel Althamer, Cezary Bodzianowski, Ulla von Brandenburg, Jeremy Deller, Trisha Donnelly, Geoffrey Farmer, Andrea Fraser, Dominique Gonzalez-Foerster, Jeppe Hein, Renata Lucas, Rita McBride, Roman Ondák, Markus Schinwald, Tino Sehgal, Catherine Sullivan and Mario Ybarra Jr. have engaged seriously with the theme of the show and offered nuanced and relevant responses.

In addition to the artists, many others have helped to realise *The World as a Stage* and we would like to thank in particular the following: Foksal Gallery, Warsaw; Produzentengalerie, Hamburg; Air de Paris, Paris; Casey Kaplan, New York; Catriona Jeffries, Vancouver; Friedrich Petzel, New York; Esther Schipper, Berlin; Johann König, Berlin; 303 Gallery, New York; Luisa Strina, São Paulo; Alexander and Bonin Gallery, New York; Martin Janda, Vienna; Georg Kargl, Vienna; Jan Mot; Brussels; Johnen and Schöttle, Cologne; Catharine Bastide, Brussels; Metro Pictures, New York; and Anna Helwig, Los Angeles. Althamer's *Film* was made possible by the generous participation of Jude Law and with the help of Victoria Belfrage, Ben Jackson and Sara Keene.

At Tate Modern many people have helped to realise the exhibition but special thanks must go to Jessica Morgan and Catherine Wood for the curatorial concept; Vanessa Desclaux for tireless assistance on all stages of the project; Maeve Polkinhorn and Cliff Lauson for support in the realisation of artists' projects and the catalogue; and Rachel Taylor for her contributions to the catalogue.

The catalogue design by A Practice for Everyday Life has captured the essence of the exhibition concept and thanks go to Judith Severne for editing the volume. We are delighted that the exhibition is travelling to Boston's Institute of Contemporary Art and would like to thank Jill Medvedow, Director and Carole Anne Meehan, Curator for helping to realise this association.

This exhibition would not have been possible without the support of Helen Thorpe, whose generous contribution towards the project of Pawel Althamer made this essential piece possible. An inspired collaboration with Platform for Art has enabled the wide dissemination of Althamer's *Film* and funding from Kirk Radke, Paulo Albert Weyland Vieira, Canada House Arts Trust, Polish Cultural Institute, Goethe-Institut London and the French Institute London has made possible many aspects of the exhibition for which we are most grateful.

Vicente Todolí
Director, Tate Modern

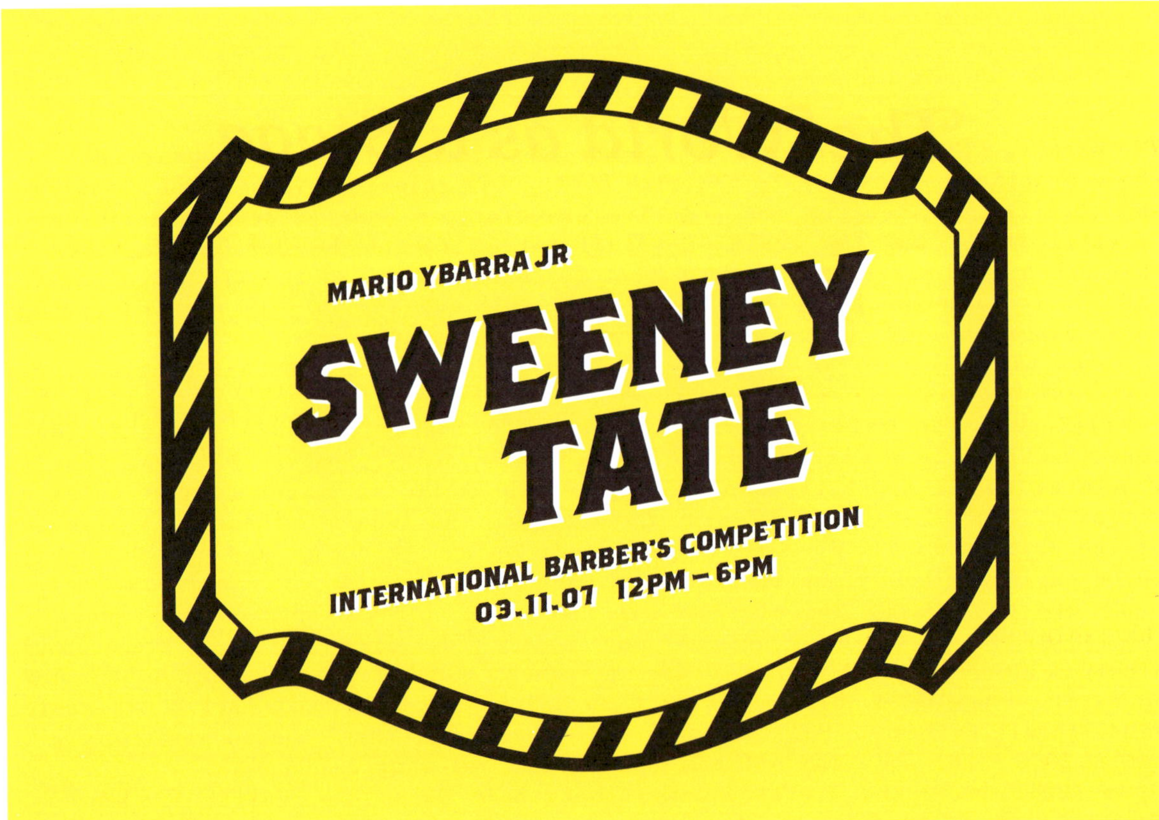
MARIO YBARRA JR
SWEENEY TATE
INTERNATIONAL BARBER'S COMPETITION
03.11.07 12PM – 6PM

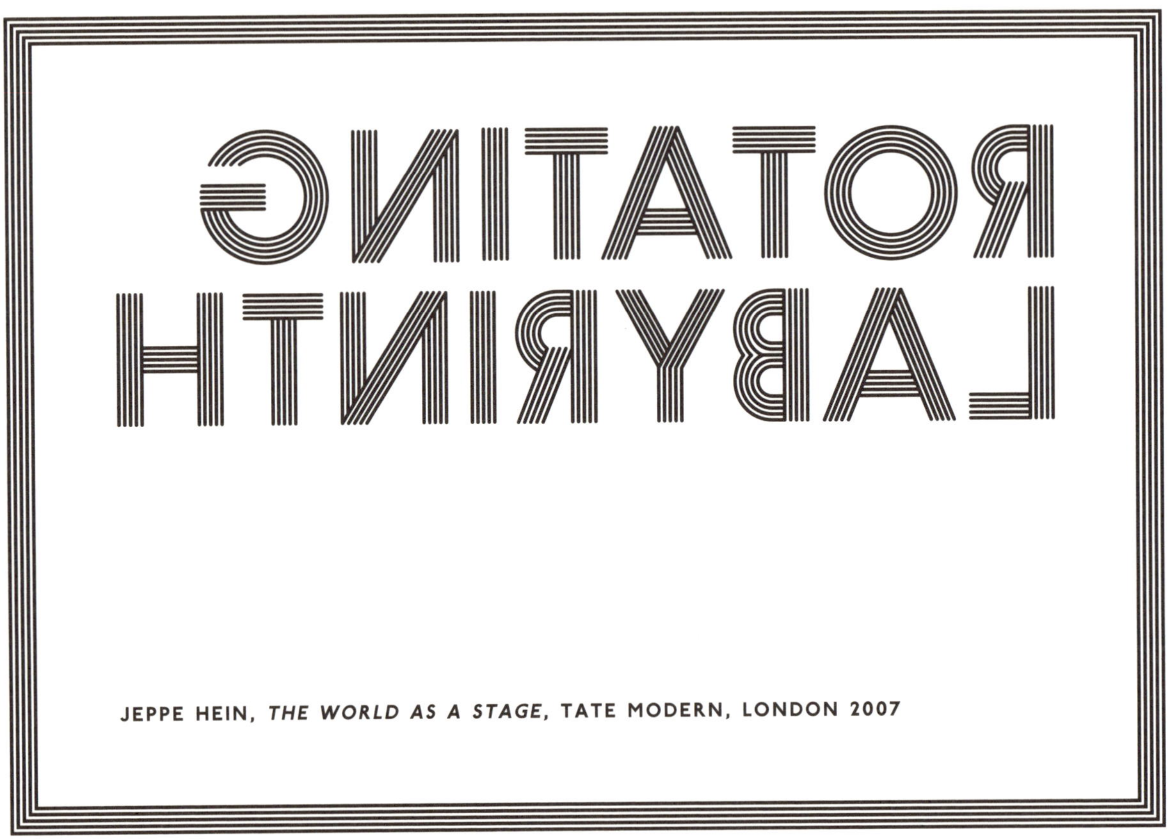
ROTATING LABYRINTH
JEPPE HEIN, *THE WORLD AS A STAGE*, TATE MODERN, LONDON 2007

The World as a Stage

CAST

Pawel Althamer, Cezary Bodzianowskí, Ulla von Brandenburg, Jeremy Deller, Trisha Donnelly, Geoffrey Farmer, Andrea Fraser, Dominique Gonzalez-Foerster, Jeppe Hein, Renata Lucas, Rita McBride, Roman Ondák, Markus Schinwald, Tino Sehgal, Catherine Sullivan, Mario Ybarra Jr.

PROLOGUE

The exhibition is a play in several acts that takes place over a number of months and in a variety of locations, both inside Tate Modern and in the world beyond. It is inspired in part by its location – London – and the city's theatrical tradition, as well as by Tate Modern's proximity to the Globe Theatre and the museum's own highly theatricalised architecture. *The World as a Stage* brings together sixteen artists whose works contain reference to acts and performances previously staged, or suggest a setting and frame that invites or even co-opts the visitor to witness or perform. Within the exhibition, different tropes of theatre – back stage, front-of-house, actors, props and audience – are placed in a dialectical relationship to the customs of art and exhibition making – studio, gallery, artist, object and viewer – so that the two realms speak about or occasionally against each other. Reality and its representation, the creation of other worlds, the use of time in space and the complex relationship between viewer and viewed are all addressed in a variety of works that make apparent the rich history of the relationship between theatre and the visual arts.

The distinction between the theatrical and the real in contemporary life has drastically atrophied over the last decades. Popular culture has embraced and sustained this lack of distinction through endless variations of 'reality' TV programming, and as a result, the public consciousness of a constructed and performed everyday extends to the perception of current social and political events. From the micro (the staging of celebrity culture) to the macro (the perception of global corporate domination and its impact on the major developments of our time), the contemporary environment seems to be an elaborate facade, and one by which we increasingly allow ourselves to be enthralled. Each change of scenery, each new act, offers a more elaborately constructed mirage in which to project oneself. Our contemporary world is arguably one immense performance, with the tragic variations that exist within it articulated by the players' ability to perceive their roles.

The World as a Stage highlights the plight of the individual in this spectacularised society, offering the dramatised and staged as a potential critique, rehearsal or analysis of our search for an understanding of our place and position in the world.

SUMMARY OF THE PLAY

Act 1.1: A London cinema
Pawel Althamer
Among the trailers preceding the main attraction is one unlike the rest. The well-known actor Jude Law appears in a London market setting; nothing in particular happens (there are some passers-by, he buys a fish), while his soliloquy suggests an introspective process of realisation, perhaps the aftermath of an unusual or transforming experience. At the end of the trailer, the audience is directed to a location rather than to a cinema: 'Experience Realtime Movie. 30 November 2007, 11.30 a.m. Borough Market ...'. Later, the audience will see further advertisements announcing the time and date of the event.

Act 1.2: The front lawn of Tate Modern
Renata Lucas
The orderly placement of birch trees in the rectangular flowerbeds of Tate's waterside garden has been disrupted by the appearance of an untamed forest. Migrating across the lawn, these intruders recklessly ignore the limits of the flowerbeds and appear to be moving towards the museum itself. A motley group of firs, pines and undergrowth, the trees may have arrived by boat and appear to be cannibalising the local plants.

Act 2.1: At the entrance to the exhibition
Tino Sehgal
The exchange of a ticket with the gallery guard results in an unexpected announcement: 'Abuse and incompetence in fight against global warming.' A conversation ensues between the guard and the puzzled visitor, who does not know if this statement is the personal opinion of the invigilator, a newspaper headline, or a statement about global warming. A month later, a different guard states: 'Revealed: the man who took Camilla's virginity.' This time, the guard is unwilling to discuss the announcement further.

Act 2.2: In the gallery
Roman Ondák
Numerous drawings show a man standing in various spaces that resemble the galleries of Tate Modern, emptied of the art. Though all the images are by different hands, the subject appears similar in each. All are portraits of the artist Roman Ondák, made by amateur artists on the basis of a description given to them by the exhibition's curators. The wall label reads: 'Roman Ondák, *I'm just acting in it* 2007'. This ambiguous title implies that those who made the drawings are the real authors of the piece, or is perhaps intended to draw attention to the entire exhibition as a staged event in which we are all performers, playing our various roles as dictated by habit and routine.

Act 2.3
Jeppe Hein, Rita McBride (back turned to the audience, identity uncertain)
The visitor approaches a mirrored theatre in the round by Jeppe Hein. Seen from the exterior, the structure disappears as the mirrored surface reflects the surrounding artworks and architecture. Once inside, the curved walls of mirrored pillars slowly align so that the rest of the gallery space is obscured. The disorienting reflective interior multiplies and simultaneously fractures the viewer, causing physical as well as visual instability. Inside the mirrored stage, one is at once actor and audience, viewer and viewed, but the incomplete and fluctuating image does not allow for any adjustment of one's role. In a further disorientation,

the movement of the curved walls means that one exits the piece from a different location into another part of the exhibition space, recalling the anxiety produced by a children's carousel as it comes to halt at a different point, with new landmarks and unfamiliar adults waiting.

Act 3.1: In the Collection display
Andrea Fraser
Something appears to have gone wrong with a multimedia guide to the Tate Collection. Instead of providing an interactive tour through the Collection with audio, related images and information, the content has taken on a life of its own. The gradually escalating sound of instructive and informational voices develops into dissonance, and the accompanying images open up on screen into a layered montage of twentieth-century art, history and popular culture. Our search for order and meaning is met with a chaotic overload of indiscernible noises and images.

INTERLUDE

Trisha Donnelly
In front of a redwood tree an older woman performs the dance *The Raven.*

Act 3.2: In the gallery
Mario Ybarra Jr.
A barber's shop has opened up in the gallery space, complete with checkerboard floor tiles, mirror and barbershop chairs. The entrance is marked by the archetypical barber's striped red and white pole, and, in a humorous twist on the homicidal London barber, a sign identifying the establishment as 'Sweeney Tate'. While the barber is missing and there are no clients, the shop has all of the cultural artifacts that accompany such sites: magazines, waiting area, images of hairstyles. The installation suggests an anthropological study into the significance of the barber's shop within various cultural and ethnic groups: a place of shared interests, group affiliation, and even social and political discussion.

Act 3.3
Ulla von Brandenburg
A *tableau vivant* is staged in a garden setting and recorded on film. The image of the event is distorted, since it has been filmed as reflected in the curved surface of a mirror ball – the sort used in gardens to scare off birds. The artist and her camera can be seen reflected in the ball, but the garden in which the scene takes place, visible around the edge of the mirror ball, remains undistorted. This layering of perceptual devices – real/representational, still/moving – is further confused by the pose and dress of the participants. Their attitudes and clothing are neither specifically of the nineteenth century, an age associated with this mode of *tableau vivant*, and nor strictly contemporary. A peculiar limbo state exists between time, movement and space, exacerbated by the endless loop of the film reel.

Act 4.1: The Globe Theatre, Bankside
Cezary Bodzianowski on a cherry picker
Walking along the waterfront adjacent to Tate Modern, visitors linger outside the historic recreation of the original site of Shakespearean London: the Globe Theatre. Strangely, the action today appears to be taking place on the exterior of the rounded space of the Globe, where attention is focused on a man intently measuring the faceted surface of the building. Each section of the exterior, as delineated by the wooden beams on the facade, is being measured to calculate the total surface area of the Globe. These results will then be compared to the total surface area

of the other globe, the world. We await the result of this analysis, perhaps wondering if the true significance of the Globe resides on the outside of the building, rather than in the interior performance space.

Act 5.1: A field in Yorkshire
Jeremy Deller
Nearly twenty years after the violent 1984 battle between Britain's striking miners and the police, Jeremy Deller restaged the event. Part historical re-enactment, part revisionist history, it culminated in a cavalry charge through the village of Orgreave. A turning point in the history of Thatcher's Britain, the miner's strike, which lasted for more than a year, is revisited in an attempt to establish the after-effects of this tumultuous period. What does it mean to restage the recent past? Quite unlike the process of projection, fantasy and conservatism associated with most historical re-enactments, *The Battle of Orgreave* is an act of rewriting history by those who were involved in the original events.

INTERVAL

Ulla von Brandenburg
A curtain closes, not quite meeting in the middle. It is a reconstruction of the patchwork curtain designed for the Royal Shakespeare Theatre in Stratford-upon-Avon. It is uncertain which side of the divide we are on – stage or front-of house. Are we performers or audience?

Act 6.1: A forest
Geoffrey Farmer
A bell rings in a forest in Exeter.

Act 6.2: In the gallery
Geoffrey Farmer
A bell rope hangs from a supporting structure. The bell itself sits oddly disconnected from this mechanism on the floor. Also in the room is a container that opens like a book. Inside it is Geoffrey Farmer's *Hunchback Kit*, an accumulation of objects or props for use in 'conceptual adaptations' of Victor Hugo's novel *Notre-Dame of Paris*. The kit contains various objects: a monk's robe, a pair of cardboard shoes for someone with a club foot and a manual that guides the reader through the various ways in which the work might be installed. As the manual makes clear, the work allows for a degree of freedom in assembly: the objects inside can be displayed – that is, staged – in radically different ways with each presentation. The rope (and the unheard bell) alludes to the bell rung by Hugo's hunchback, Quasimodo.

Act 7.1
Rita McBride (this time facing audience), Catherine Sullivan
Quite unexpectedly, we find our position in the exhibition reversed: confronted by the proscenium seating of Rita McBride's *Arena*, we are suddenly on stage, and the scattering of people seated on the bleachers watch our entrance. At this time, it is up to us either to perform or to observe, but advertisements in the guide announce *Arena's* future incarnation as a platform for various live events.

An adjacent projected video shows what appears to be a theatrical rehearsal. The actors seem to belong to a variety of different performances, as suggested by their anachronistic costumes, which indicate both nineteenth- and twentieth-century dress, and incongruous characters including a priest, a secretary, and a rock star. It is unclear in the cacophony of sound and movement if the members of the motley group are practising their parts, responding to directions, or actually performing their roles. The actors seem forever stuck in a limited repertoire of prescribed attitudes, gestures and noises, even the tempo of which they are unable to vary.

INTERLUDE

Trisha Donnelly
The Raven continues.

Act 7.2: Next to Arena
Pawel Althamer, Markus Schinwald
Under the bleachers of *Arena* is a pile of clothing; hanging nearby is a mannequin. These seem to be props or costumes from an earlier performance. The clothing is that of a businessman, complete with briefcase, mobile phone and wallet, apparently abandoned in a swift change of role and left as evidence of the 'act'. The mannequin has an oddly lifelike face, and its body twitches slightly in a repetitive, threatening movement from which it seems unable to break loose.

Act 8.1: Exiting the gallery
Dominique Gonzalez-Foerster
Drawn to the blue glow of a corridor-like space, the visitor finds that bright lights are triggered on entering. Ghostly shadows of oneself and others are projected onto the blue-painted wall. These shadow performers glide out of the exhibition space in an ethereal, almost televisual realm.

Final Act: Borough Market 11.30 a.m., 30 November 2007
Pawel Althamer
Crowds have gathered to see the new Jude Law film advertised to take place this morning. Searching for a screen, the actors, or any evidence of the advertised film, the audience begins to recognise both the setting (Borough Market) and the extras that appeared in the trailer (a jogger, a tourist, an older woman and her son). Passers-by may be mistaken for Jude Law, who is rumoured to be there, and confusion remains as to the action. Has the film started? Has it ended? Some people may catch sight of Jude Law, who enters a shop, buys a fish, and leaves.

All Exeunt

Jessica Morgan
Curator of Contemporary Art, Tate Modern

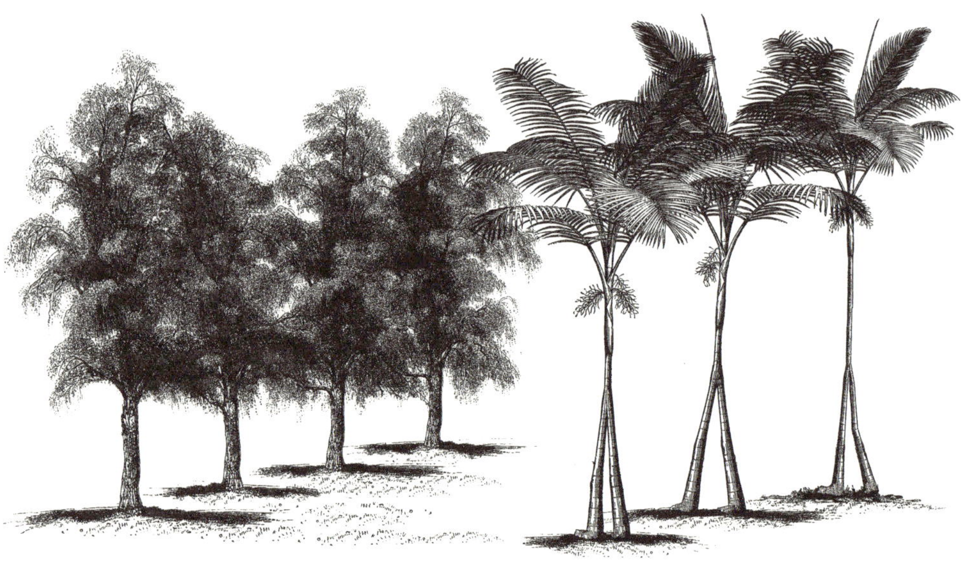

Arena

TATE MODERN
BANKSIDE
LONDON SE1

THE WORLD AS A STAGE

27 OCTOBER 2007 16.00 – 21.00

ARENA DISCOTECA FLAMING STAR CATRIONA SHAW TAPE MISS LE BOMB
RITA MCBRIDE FRANÇOIS BOUÉ LENTEJAS MICHAEL MAHALCHICK
BEADSWOLFGANG MAYER BENE ABEL GLEN RUBSAMENN PROTEA GINA
ARENA CRISTINA GOMEZ BARRIO CABLES SURPRISING SURPRISES GB

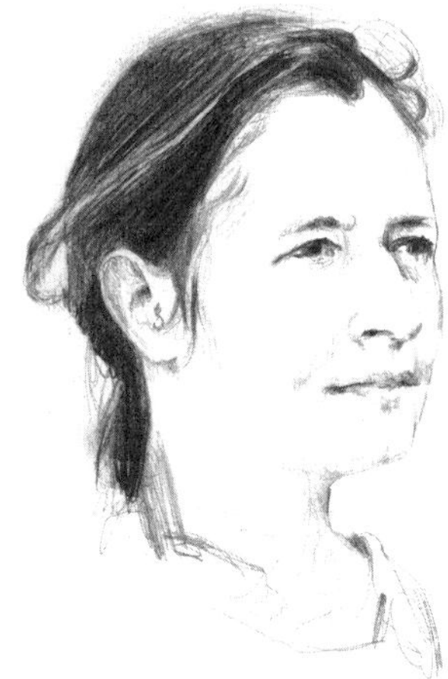

Dominique Gonzalez-Foerster

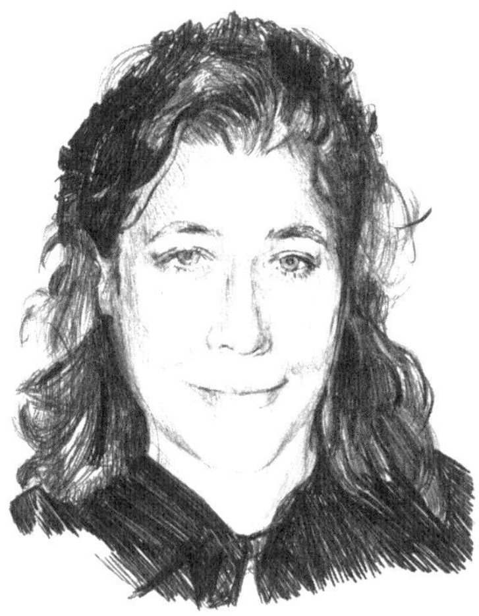

Rita McBride

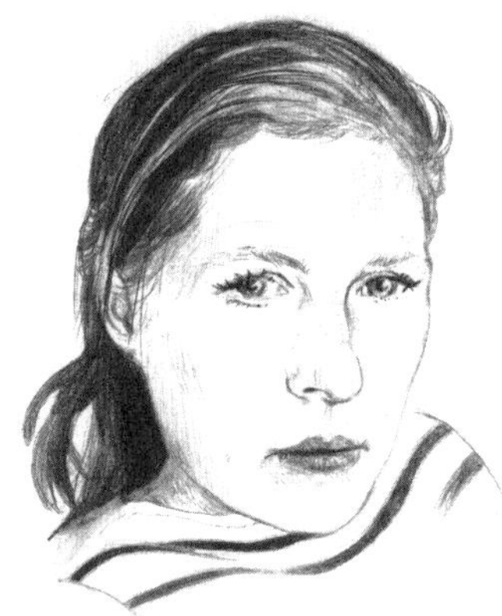

Ulla von Brandenburg

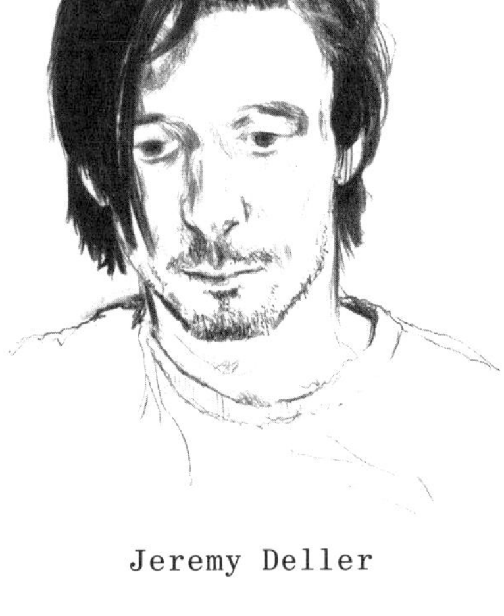

Jeremy Deller

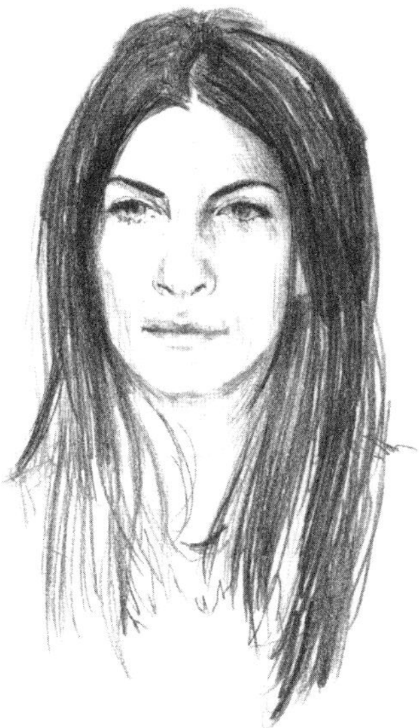

Trisha Donnelly

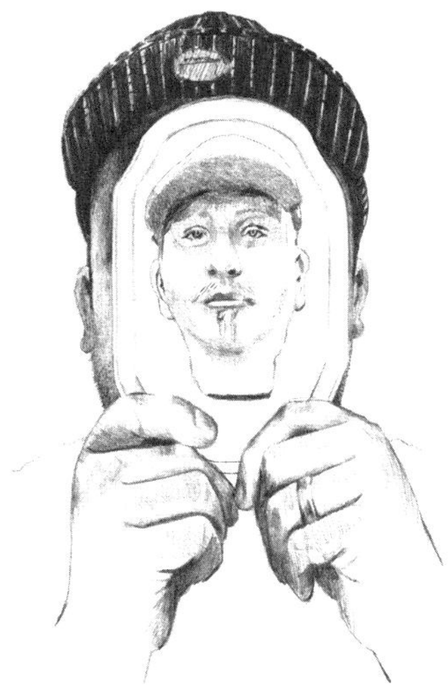

Mario Ybarra Jr.

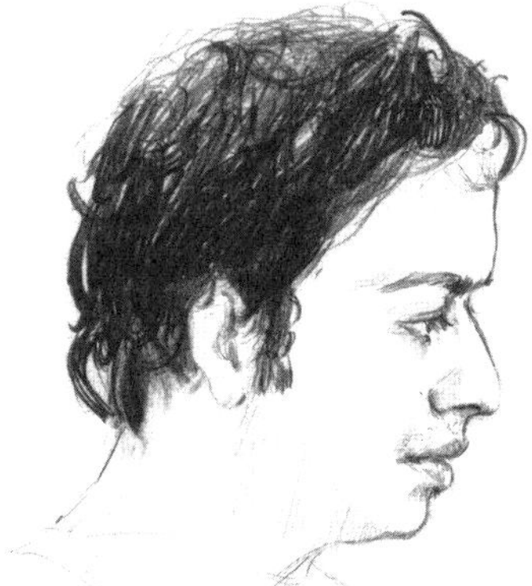

Tino Sehgal

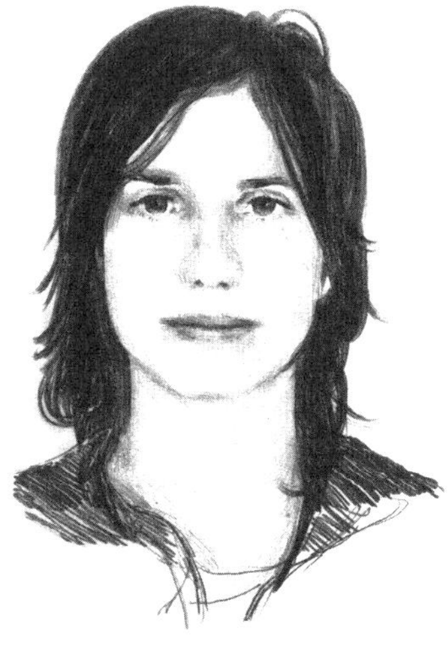

Renata Lucas

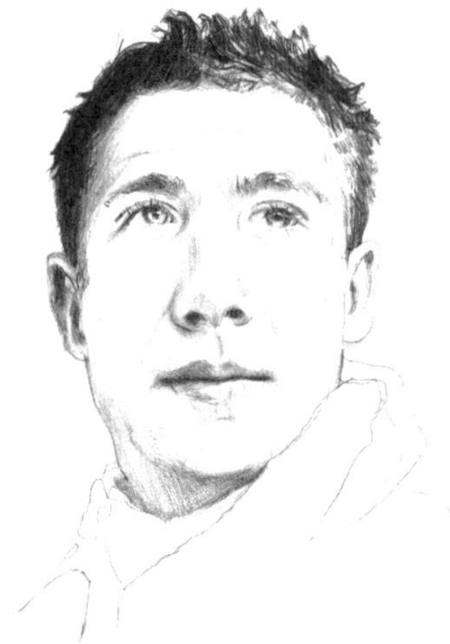

Jeppe Hein

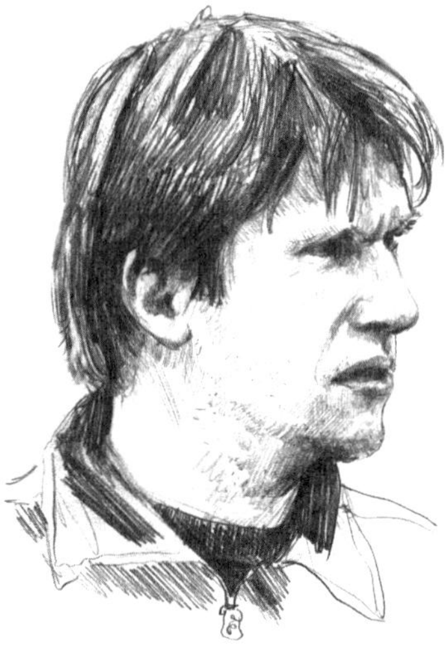

Roman Ondák

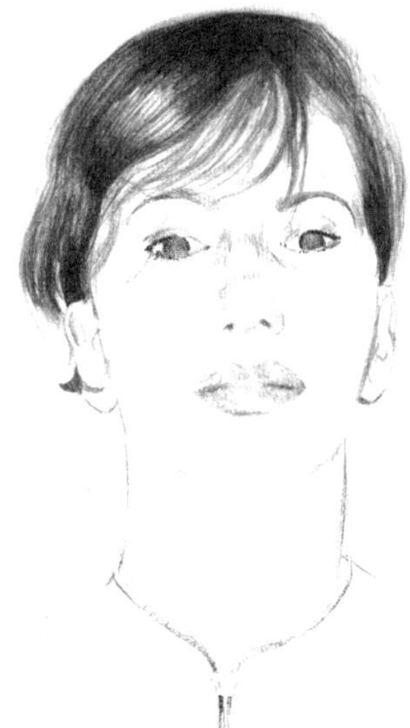

Andrea Fraser

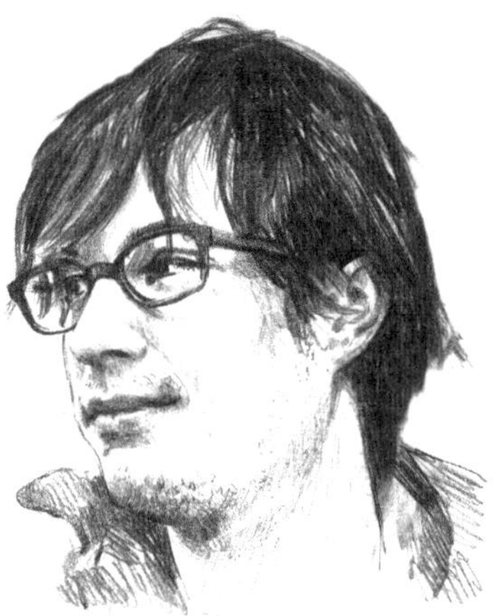

Markus Schinwald

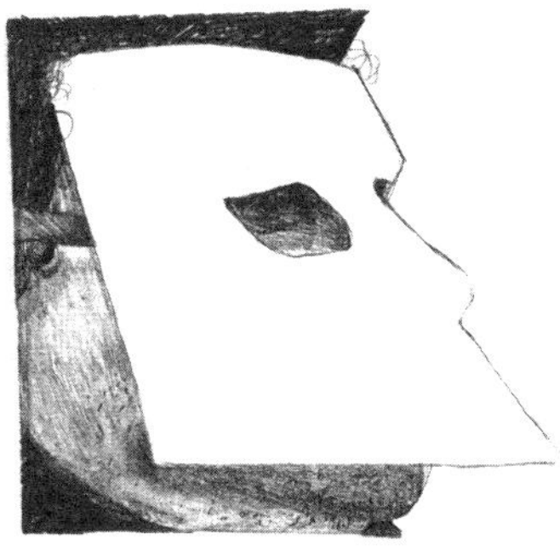

Cezary Bodzianowski

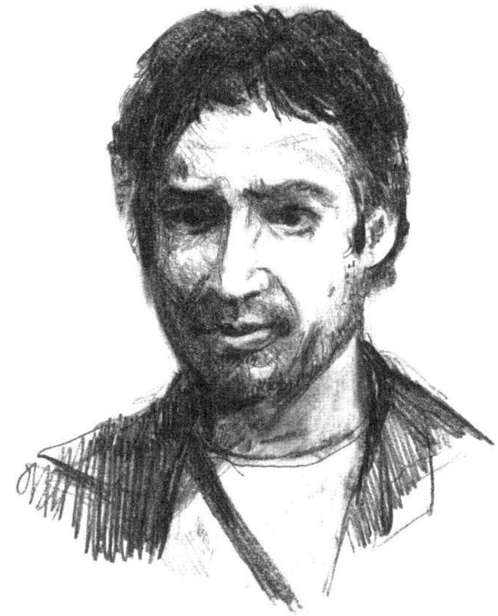

Pawel Althamer

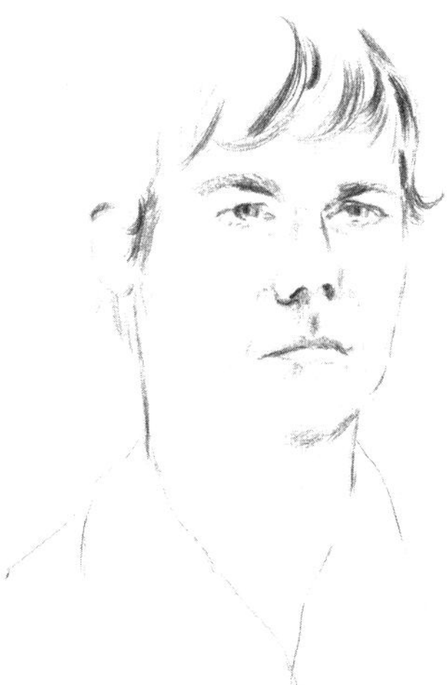

Geoffrey Farmer

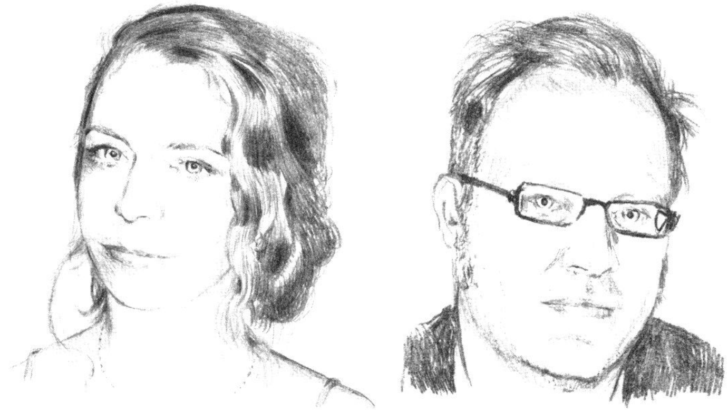

Catherine Sullivan & Sean Griffin

Art Meets Theatre: The Middle Zone

I. FOUR WALLS / FOURTH WALL

'Theatricality' was, more or less, a forbidden zone in twentieth-century art practice. The foundations of modernism were built upon a vocabulary of logic, rigour, revelation of process; epitomised by Frank Stella's 'What you see is what you see'.[1] The champion of high-modernist painting, Michael Fried, notoriously declared in 1967 that theatre was art's outright 'enemy'.[2] But a contradictory fantasy of 'theatre' combining the revelation of its mechanics in the work of Bertold Brecht[3] with a return to its pre-modern 'magic', championed by Antonin Artaud, has slowly begun to surface in the contemporary artistic imagination. This is a wilful historical conflation that foregrounds theatre's active constitution by people configured in spectatorial relations and, at the same time, brings to mind a whole other aesthetic lexicon: of enchantment, exaggeration, absurdity, artificiality, the suspension of disbelief. The works in *The World as a Stage* are brought together in an attempt to consider the renewed appeal of the notion of 'theatre' for a significant number of artists working today. In diverse ways, these works challenge the exclusions brought about by the analytical logic of modernism; they do so through the invocation of ritual, suggestion and immersion in altered modes of perception of space and time, and through a lack of anxiety about fixing the boundaries of their discipline.

The art historian Benjamin Buchloh has analysed modernism's 'phobic prohibition' of theatricality in terms of a repression of pictoriality. He wrote that modernism's 'declared enemies … remained the same throughout the twentieth century: historical narrativity, figural representation, theatrical enactment – in other words, all the conventions of depiction and figuration that painting had once shared with the other arts, theatre and literature in particular.'[4] The question at the heart of *The World as a Stage* expands Buchloh's enquiry to ask: what is our relationship to the realm of representation in a situation where, due to the surveillance and reality-television inflected culture in which we live, the parameters of 'the represented' and the roles of actor or spectator do not clearly begin or end? Though the artwork itself might include discrete objects or 'pictures', its representational field is always an expanded one. This expanded field is founded upon, or implies, an understanding of the ritualised relationships between people that lend objects or images significance. It is not only theatre's grounding in narrative and fiction, but its explicit reliance upon the co-presence of actor and spectator that defines its difference from art, and offers it as an alternative model of practice. The aesthetic imagination that is at play here foregrounds the intentional relationships that form culture. That is to say, it is built upon an anthropological basis rather than making claims for art occupying a fixed and quasi-spiritual, transcendent sphere.

To embrace theatre is, then, at one level, to open up an anthropologically oriented alternative to the dominant twentieth-century model of gallery practice as it was defined by Brian O'Doherty in *Inside the White Cube*. O'Doherty demonstrated how the convention of the white-walled gallery as a timeless and 'pure' space for showing art framed human presence as a grotesque intrusion. Rather than being a necessary witness here, the spectator 'stumbles' clumsily about with an out-of-place physicality. It was precisely this foregrounding of bodily presence within a durational context without a clear beginning or ending point to which Fried objected. The modernist realm was better suited, O'Doherty wryly observes, to the all-seeing but disembodied notion of the 'Eye': the impossible, ideal viewing position. Installation shots of this work are typically spectator-free, he notes.

In contrast to the apparent immanence of the white-cube space, theatre is a form of ritual that is necessarily embedded in the temporal reality of life. Durkheim identified theatre as being derived from the oldest forms of religious or spiritual ceremonial, which themselves were the ways in which a society would initiate and reinforce cultural beliefs, in a manner that was collectively witnessed. In the 1920s, German theatre theorist Max Herrmann wrote that 'the original meaning of theatre was derived from the fact that it was a social game – played by all for all. A game in which everyone is a player – participants and spectators.'[5] As a conceptual notion, theatre contains an extreme capacity for dispersal and portability. As Peter Brook wrote in 1968, 'I can take any empty space and call it a bare stage. A man walks across this empty space whilst someone else is watching him, and this is all that is needed for an act of theatre to be engaged.'[6] Yet whilst the 'white cube' represses the theatrical nature of its staging of a neutral blankness as a backdrop for art, the theatre, as Brook observes, has traditionally come with an array of ritualised conventions: 'red curtains, spotlights, blank verse, laughter, darkness'.[7] The legacy of these 'trappings' – whether they are literally used by modern theatre directors or not – is that the mention of 'theatre' evokes a hypnotic atmosphere of potential magic and transformation that identifies its realm as a liminal space in which we expect something to happen. 'Theatre' is a space that requires our participation as witnesses, and yet it is a space in which we might lose ourselves by suspending our logical faculties in favour of its fiction.

The reintroduction of the capacities of the theatre as a space in which to expand art practice opens up new territory not only beyond the immutability of high modernism, but also beyond work made in direct opposition to that mode, such as that characterised by Nicholas Bourriaud in terms of 'relational aesethetics'. This work deliberately framed the spectator's actual presence as a part of the piece, requiring audiences to eat a meal, for instance, go down a slide or commune under a 'discussion platform' to complete the intended picture. Broadly speaking, the artists in *The World as a Stage* create a different kind of space that lies between two representational modes, colliding the white cube's four walls and the theatre's 'fourth wall' to stretch the representational zone into a potentially borderless dimension of pervasive theatricality. The resulting work effects a temporally extended, habitable sphere for art that in its virulent penetration of the viewer's own perception moves beyond any literal notion of physical 'participation'. Bringing the subject's de-centred and spatial experience of the art installation between and beyond the four walls of the gallery into dialogue with the planar image offered by the proscenium theatre or installation shot's ideal viewpoint, this work creates scenarios that deliberately muddle literal presence with the possibilities offered by the aesthetic imagination, mixing direct experience and representation.

In this sense, the work renegotiates not only the status of the art object but also the image plane as a site of activity, in opposition to Guy Debord's characterisation of the capitalist 'spectacle' as 'alienating screen'. Extending a lineage that connects with historical predecessors including Yvonne Rainer, Dan Graham, James Coleman, Cindy Sherman, Guy de Cointet and Mike Kelley, such work challenges the continuum that Buchloh identifies as linking the 'purism' of high modernist abstraction with the 'transparency' of a documentary use of new media. Invoking 'theatre' gives a certain permission to play. The reintroduction of forbidden dimensions of art practice inflected by fiction invites things to get a little more fantastical, and a little less constrained by an art-historical narrative of progressiveness.[8] Mike Kelley said of his figurative sculpture exhibition *The Uncanny* – which doubled the idea of the 'return' in a Freudian sense – that this kind of staged scenario offers illicit permission to 'play with dead things'. The artists gathered here might be said to muddle the dead and the living, mixing live-ness with stasis, subject with object, entrenched convention with unpredictability. In all of this, the boundaries between the art object and fluid reality are opened up to such an extent that to engage with the work means to enter a performative, paranoid, enchanted world that reflects upon and refuses the nature of contemporary reality in equal measure.

II. LIVING OBJECTS, LIVING PICTURES

A dynamic tension between movement and fixity connects works in the exhibition. For the subject, this means testing the notion of acting as rehearsed repetition against acting as spontaneous agency; for the object, it means testing its status as an encounter against its facticity as a discrete 'thing'. The notion of a fluid field of representation is investigated in the interventionist works of Pawel Althamer, Roman Ondák and Tino Sehgal. Emblematic of the exhibition's concept in its widest sense, Althamer's *Film* is a piece of real-time theatre occurring as everyday action in the street that is advertised in advance via an apparently authentic cinema trailer. *Film* speaks of 'the world as a stage' at many levels, but most significant is the way in which it initiates raised perceptual awareness of the inherent theatricality of life in the spectators, who are also framed as participants, and at the same time injects the ordinary scene with narrative fiction, by blurring it with the glamour of Hollywood, embodied in the presence of actor Jude Law. The way in which *Film* blurs everyday activity with representation is characteristic of the extent to which a sense of 'theatricality' has, in recent practice, become invested in the perception of the art viewer over and above being a quality of the object itself; a self-reflexive mode carried beyond the parameters of the gallery environment in which it was initiated.

Significantly, though Althamer's piece is in material form closer to theatre than to cinema, it is named after the medium that is undoubtedly contemporary culture's dominant vehicle of representation. This paradoxical choice of title indicates a resistance to 'spectacle' culture by reclaiming the two-dimensional image as a space to inhabit, creating a 'situation' that could be, as in Debord's conception, a potential counter to 'the image'. In the development of the expanded situation of installation art during the years in which Debord was writing, and since, it might be said that the experiential space of this new form of art situated the viewer *within* the representational realm. In *Film*, the actors who have featured in the cinema trailer perform their scripted actions within a spatial scene, telling a story that by dint of its unfolding in real space and time cannot possibly resemble the flat linearity of the narrative mode of conventional cinema. The effect of this for the viewer, turning this way and that in an attempt to perceive the 'film', is that the image-plane cuts through real life in multiple, criss-crossing planes of intersection, dissolving the status of the image as a 'screen' and instead instigating a field of heightened, activated perception that has no clear beginning or end; no indication of which side we might be on. In this way, the entire scene becomes infused with a sense of artificiality and play-acting, within which one perceives, perhaps with alarm, one's own participation. The situations orchestrated by Sehgal, such as *This is New* 2003 or *This is Propaganda* 2002, operate in a similar way within the conventions of the gallery or museum; inserting scripted episodes into the apparently 'neutral' staffing structure to elicit the potential disruption of expected patterns of person-to-person behaviour and exchange. Ondak's instruction pieces performed by actors, such as his 'queue' titled *Good Feelings in Good Times* 2003, choreograph a form of invisible sculpture that is embedded almost imperceptibly within the everyday.

In contrast to these limitless situations, Ulla von Brandenburg, Markus Schinwald, Catherine Sullivan and Trisha Donnelly stage the dilemma of representation as a moment of stasis straining against life's mobility. Von Brandenburg is fascinated by the explicit marking of beginnings and endings. Her theatrical *tableaux vivants*, either posed for film or presented as live performances, often exaggerate the moment of the curtain being pulled back as an explicit theatrical convention. The curtain piece displayed within this exhibition petrifies that moment, stilling either the opening or the closing of a play, with extended ambiguity. Within her film work, live presence is frequently figured as stillness in a protracted moment of ending. It is as though her characters attempt to inhabit the image plane by becoming simultaneous with it. In von Brandenburg's work, the viewer is cast quite clearly in the role of spectator, yet her performers are never fully possessed by the spectator's vision: we see them wobble or move slightly, so that the seamlessness of the representation is broken, dramatising a compelling tension between their individuality and their cooperative participation as a work of art.

Catherine Sullivan's work is also a form of *tableau vivant*, albeit one for the television age. Her actors repeat clipped, stuttering gestures in endless patterns, gestures that might communicate emotion or dialogue if they were not removed from any sense of narrative succession. Trisha Donnelly's *Redwood and the Raven* presents a different kind of 'film', as a one-frame-per-day dance for camera; a ritual that can only be witnessed through repeat visits. The choreography incorporates 'real life' by dint of this temporal structure: the viewer's reading of the photographed dancer's movement sequence will necessarily be interrupted by the pedestrian movement of real life that is sandwiched in between its stalled snapshot-by-snapshot progression. Markus Schinwald's mannequin, by contrast, effects a disturbance of perception by performing unexpected occasional movements that uncannily disrupt its status as object sculpture.

A recent work by Cezary Bodzianowski, which is not in the exhibition, links these experiments with theatre as either boundary-less movement or performed stasis. For a piece made in Cologne in May 2007, Bodzianowski invited his audience to meet at a certain point at the advertised time of 3.00p.m and walk to find him in the city street. A small crowd gathered around the point at which he was positioned; he stood at the side of the road as though about to cross it, but remained completely still. After a while, the stopped rudimentary digital clock once telling the time as a part of a long-faded Phillips 'new technology' advert on the building opposite came into focus, directed by the artist's gaze towards it. Like Bodzianowski, it did not move forwards from 3.00 p.m. Both were temporarily petrified in an extended moment of immobility: in time, amid the busy city street, and yet outside of it; a conflation of sculpture and theatre. In this simple act, as with his other actions, Bodzianowski created an absurd and compelling image within the everyday from the most economical of means.

The question of whether acting is 'live' or repeated, and therefore fixed, is also central to works by Jeremy Deller and Andrea Fraser. Deller's invitation in 2002 to the original participants in the 'Battle of Orgreave' to re-enact history by working with a combination of re-enactment enthusiasts and original participants created an extraordinary cultural ritual of representation and reiteration. Although the real narrative history was played out, its live-ness did not necessarily reinforce what had happened but made visible a sense of its fragile contingency, incorporating the sense, within the moment of its enacting, that somehow the outcome might be different. Nevertheless, Deller described the re-enactment in terms of re-living the past whilst fully acknowledging its past-ness, saying, 'if anything, it was about digging up a hastily buried corpse and giving it a proper post-mortem.'[9] The archive installation in the show might be seen as an expansion of this process, incorporating it into the ritualistic space of the museum.

Conversely, Fraser doubles the 'acted-ness' of the roles she assumes to the point of often comical exaggeration. For *Official Welcome* 2001, originally presented by the MICA Foundation at a private reception and reperformed as a part of the Whitechapel Art Gallery's *Short History of Performance*, she undermined the notion of authentic bodily presence associated with the naked female 'performance artist' by staging her 'act' as a repeatable, sellable one. Mimicking a speech from an art-awards ceremony while stripping down to her underwear she concluded, 'I am not a person today. I'm an object in an art work.' For Tate, she has created a piece that inhabits the interpretative voice of the institution's multimedia guide, scrambling its didactic approach to art history in order to transform it into a space of play that randomly conjures new, often incongruous, narratives.

Sculpture or installation as a form of 'stage-set' framing the spectator is played out variously in the works by Jeppe Hein, Dominique Gonzalez-Foerster, Geoffrey Farmer, Mario Ybarra, Rita McBride and Renata Lucas. These pieces in very different ways create liminal spaces or interventions that disorient, or re-orient, perception: by simultaneously immersing and staging the viewer in a mirrored maze or environment of coloured light; by causing an improbable rupture in the familiar landscape in front of the museum; by recreating a fully functioning barber's shop inside the gallery to stage its activity as a cultural ritual of performative masculinity; or by proposing an installation of sculpture as a 'kit' comprising props as prompts for thought, loosely tied by their invitation to the viewer to imaginatively reconstruct a well-known narrative.

If Althamer's *Film* is the clearest investigation of dispersed theatrical representation in the everyday, Rita McBride's *Arena* is the exhibition's anchor. The large-scale sculpture, which is built both to resemble and function as stadium seating, marks the most explicit axis of back-and-forth negotiation in the exhibition's investigation of spectator dynamics. *Arena* invites viewers to sit on its tiered seats, from which point they simultaneously complete its appearance as an arena and sit in a position in which they can view others, who, upon entering the sculpture's space, appear as though they are on stage. *Arena* is also used to stage performance events by other artists. Von Brandenburg's, McBride's and Althamer's works might be taken as three triangulation points that orientate us within the expansive territory of the show: territory that links image, object and embodied perception in the evocation of a theatrical zone.

III. ART AS A DIMENSION OF ACTION

In the early twentieth century, Russian Constructivist artists such as Alexander Rodchenko and Varvara Stepanova imagined the revolutionary potential of their abstract art forms via the creation of not only painting and sculpture but also the applied arts in costumes for workers, furniture, ceramics and graphic design.

They also made props, costumes and sets for theatre. For the play *The Death of Tarelkin* (1922), Vsevolod Meyerhold invited Stepanova to design costumes and also to create 'acting apparatuses' as combined props/furniture/settings to be manipulated by the actors. Rodchenko designed costumes and props for a number of theatre productions including *Bed Bug* in 1929. Whilst Rodchenko said that he was representing a vision of the 'future', but very much a Constructivist, utilitarian one, a contemporary reviewer believed that *Bed Bug* 'depicted a new model of life on an almost unreal plane'.[10] What these conflicting attitudes highlight is that the theatre provided a space that conflated reality with invention in a palpably rudimentary and yet fantastical way. Though elements of Rodchenko's and Stepanova's revolutionary art and design were realised in the wider world in situations such as the USSR Workers' Club in the late 1920s, their vision for the most part remained at the level of model and design and fine art presentation. Their imagined world found its fullest manifestation in the space of the theatre, where acted scenes involving props, costumes and gestures were presented in a total environment on stage. In this way, the intended meaning of the abstract forms was somehow supplemented by a vision of their use and application, a kind of displacement of figuration played out as a passing but high-impact vision.

A similar displacement might be observed in an understanding of the significance of the Judson Theatre, and in particular Yvonne Rainer's work in relation to the contemporaneous reception of Minimalism. Minimalist-style props utilised in her dance works created scenarios that made a kind of sense of the spectator's ambiguous encounter with the blank-form sculpture of her contemporaries, such as Robert Morris, who had participated with Rainer in the dance scene. In both of these cases, participation with the 'art object' was not literally invited of the spectator, but was acted out as an imaginatively constructed *mise-en-scène*. In these scenarios, the suspended disbelief offered by the theatre stage was utilised as a utopian space that could imagine how things might – if the aesthetic and everyday sphere could be integrated – be different.[11]

The concept of 'theatre' as it has been utilised in these historic works has become a newly useful term because of the way in which it puts actor and object into a dynamic, fictionalised state of play. Though the realm of 'performance art' has been associated with a mode of non-commercial experiment that is productively at odds with the art object, the usefulness of conceiving of 'performance' as a separate area of practice becomes problematic for much contemporary work. The argument made in RoseLee Goldberg's pioneering history of the medium in the 1970s proposed that the innovation offered by performance has a role to play that might be seen to serve objects, in the sense that it feeds into transitional moments in the development of new painterly or sculptural forms and styles. Such a view, still widely held and manifested, for example, in the exhibition *Out of Actions* at the Museum of Contemporary Art, Los Angeles in 1997, sets performed action and material object in a relationship that inadvertently reinforces a hierarchy of value in favour of the status of the object as an 'outcome'. Rather than championing performance as a form of 'authentic' opposition to gallery-based art, it now makes sense to understand relations between performance and the object in terms of a theatrical situation. In other words, this is to understand their meaning in a co-dependent situation of reciprocity that fears neither the 'achieving of objecthood' for live work, nor the art object as prop or 'stage setting'. The notion of 'theatre' is useful because it presupposes the inclusion of the actor, the object, the *mise-en-scène* and the spectator as a total situation. The way in which artists in the exhibition invoke 'theatre' brings an understanding of the sculptural quality of this total situation, and at the same time understands such a notion as a pure condition of perception, meaning a willingness to buy into a different set of rules; to 'play the game'.

Such an observation prompts the question of where this game might lead. In a recent article about performance, Melanie Gilligan argues that the ideas of participation, activation and role-play that underwrite much contemporary practice cannot clearly claim political agency because they have already been appropriated by the machinations of contemporary capitalism. But if theatrical performativity is truly the all-pervasive condition at the beginning of the twenty-first century, then it is certain that there is space to consider how this condition is manipulated, by whom and to what ends. Such strategies are largely, of course, directed towards familiar, mainstream profit-making, even if there is a masquerade of 'alternative-ness' at play. Art that embraces this capacity of consciousness has the potential to insinuate itself into the mechanics of the operation, to challenge via the evocation of alternative models or fictions how and why the staged is staged, and how the apparent 'fixity' of dominant forms of representation become that way. Judith Butler's model of 'performativity' characterises the habitual repeating of character traits (associated, in the case of her argument, with the performance of gender) as a kind of 'sedimentation' of cultural norms that though essentially mobile and passing in their individual iterations become 'facts' through repetition. Butler's model is usefully applied to the broader 'norms' of culture's enactment through rehearsal and repeating. By creating an expanded zone for representation, mapping the sculptural or the pictorial onto live experience, the immutable status of all apparently fixed forms might be imaginatively challenged.

Bourriaud considered the staging of human relations in 'relational aesthetics' with reference to Marcel Mauss's *The Gift*, an anthropological text that framed ritual exchange between people in terms of the transferral and reciprocation of objects of value. An article by contemporary anthropologist David Graeber offers an alternative perspective on ritual and the object that has resonance with the status of the art object in the work of the current generation. Graeber reinterprets the significance of the 'fetish' in African tribal cultures so as to challenge our understanding of 'the commodity fetish' as it was interpreted by Marx. Looking at sixteenth-century European traders' understanding of the ascription of value to objects by their African counterparts, Graeber posits that it was based on a misunderstanding of what was truly valued within those African societies. The arbitrariness of the emblematic object that was designated as a fetish – for example 'a pot of ashes, a whisk broom, a piece of elephant bone'[13] – was, he observes, to do with the emphasis within those communities on the social contract or oath that was signified by the object over and above the inherent value of the object itself. The European obsession with material wealth and lack of interest in social relations meant that the traders blindly missed this point. Graeber believes that his revised understanding of the position of the object's status within social relations points towards a productive understanding of the locus of creativity that 'is not an aspect of the object at all', but 'a dimension of action'.[14] Even a temporarily performed image could constitute a ritual of fetish, he notes. He learns from this that, 'by a form of collective investment one can, in effect, create a new god on the spot'.[15] In the African society, Graeber observed, 'material objects were interesting mainly in so far as they became entangled in social relations, or enabled one to create new ones … It was as though everything existed in that the middle zone which the Europeans were trying to evacuate; everything was social – nothing fixed, therefore everything was both material and social simultaneously.'[16]

In this conception of things, as in much of the work in this exhibition, there is no 'finished product' or end point. The 'fetish' – or the art object – can literally be a mobile entity. This idea of the 'middle zone' is precisely what has disturbed the twentieth-century champions of the avant-garde in their respective disciplines: Brecht, in his concern that 'so long as the arts are supposed to be "fused" together, the various elements will all be equally degraded',[17] and Fried in his view that 'art degenerates as it approaches the condition of theatre'.[18] And yet it is precisely a rejection of medium-specificity that unites the artists here; a willingness to reintroduce elements of narrative, figuration, theatre and a refusal to exclude the possibilities inherent in other disciplines. Graeber speaks of this confusion of material and social, or material and spiritual, as an 'enchanted world' in which, as in the Baroque theatre, the construction of illusion was revealed at the same time as the spectacle of illusion itself was enjoyed, allowing for 'a constant process of imagining new social arrangements and then trying to bring them into being'.[19] Graeber suggests that looking back at the roots of this cultural misunderstanding might help contemporary society to see itself as, 'to some degree an intentional thing'.[20]

It is in this way that the imaginative capacity opened up by the space of theatre offers new life to contemporary art practice. Rather than thinking about art in terms of 'performance' versus 'object' or, as Jacques Rancière has discussed, active 'participation' versus passive 'spectatorship',[21] it makes sense to think in terms of Graeber's middle zone, or Tadeusz Kantor's notion that art itself is an intensified 'hole in reality, without a destination and without a place'.[22] As it has been explored by the artists in *The World as a Stage*, the theatrical middle zone proposes a genuine transferral of attention towards inter-subjective relations, revealing the blurredness of life and art via a new mode of aesthetic perception. The rudimentary grafting together of the real and the imaginary that this model implies radically revitalises our understanding of culture as a contingent and communal process of enactment.

Catherine Wood
Curator of Contemporary Art and Performance, Tate Modern

PAWEL ALTHAMER

In Pawel Althamer's work, reality and the everyday are inexhaustible sources of found theatre. His installations, sculptures and actions, as well as humorous and poetic interventions, depict unique observations of the world as he has experienced it.

In *Film* 2000–7, Althamer created a scenario for a performance advertised as a 'film' by a conventional cinema trailer. The script identified characters one might see walking down the street of any city, including a jogger, a mother and a child, a businessman or an old man reading a newspaper. This everyday situation was then acted out on the streets by performers, including a well-known actor who is the central character of *Film*. For *The World as a Stage*, a new version of *Film* will be presented in London. The trailer will invite cinema viewers to experience *Film* at Borough Market on Friday, 30 November 2007. If they turn up to see the 'film', the invited spectators might recognise some of the passers-by from the trailer, dispersed within the crowd passing through the market. The viewers might also get caught up in Althamer's illusory attempt to direct everyday life, confusing actors with real passers-by, the spectators themselves becoming part of the theatrical frame and of the real-time performance.

In works such as this, Althamer brings to the fore the acts of observing, walking or listening as ways of experiencing everyday life and engaging with the situations and people one encounters. He creates situations that expose certain groups of people and socio-economic conditions, inviting the viewers to consider them from a different perspective. In *Dancers* 1997, Althamer staged a performance with a group of homeless people, who formed a circle and danced naked in a white and brightly lit room. With *Einstein Class* 2005, he proposed to set up a physics class for a group of teenagers from a deprived neighbourhood in Warsaw, taking them on outdoor trips and to Berlin for the opening of an exhibition that marked the anniversary of Albert Einstein's death. Through those actions, Althamer challenges accepted hierarchies and logic, and proposes alternative ways of looking.

Self-portraiture also appears as a leitmotif throughout Althamer's practice. This idea is developed in works such as *Self-Portrait as a Businessman* 2002–4, in which a typical city worker's suit, wallet and briefcase are left on the floor as if their owner had just undressed and walked away; or in *Self-Portrait* 1993, a realistic life-size sculpture of Althamer's own body. The self-portrait is also investigated obliquely through the autobiographical references that often inspire his actions such as *Fairytale* 2006, an installation and real-time performance in which Althamer intended to help an illegal immigrant in Berlin to obtain legal residency in Germany. This illusory and unstable portrait of the artist points to contemporary ideas of isolation and unsettled identity, raising the spectre of the crisis of the individual. Yet, despite the serious issues his work explores, Althamer's works always subtly shift in focus between reality and fiction, drawing attention to how fine the line between darkness and lightness can be. *Vanessa Desclaux*

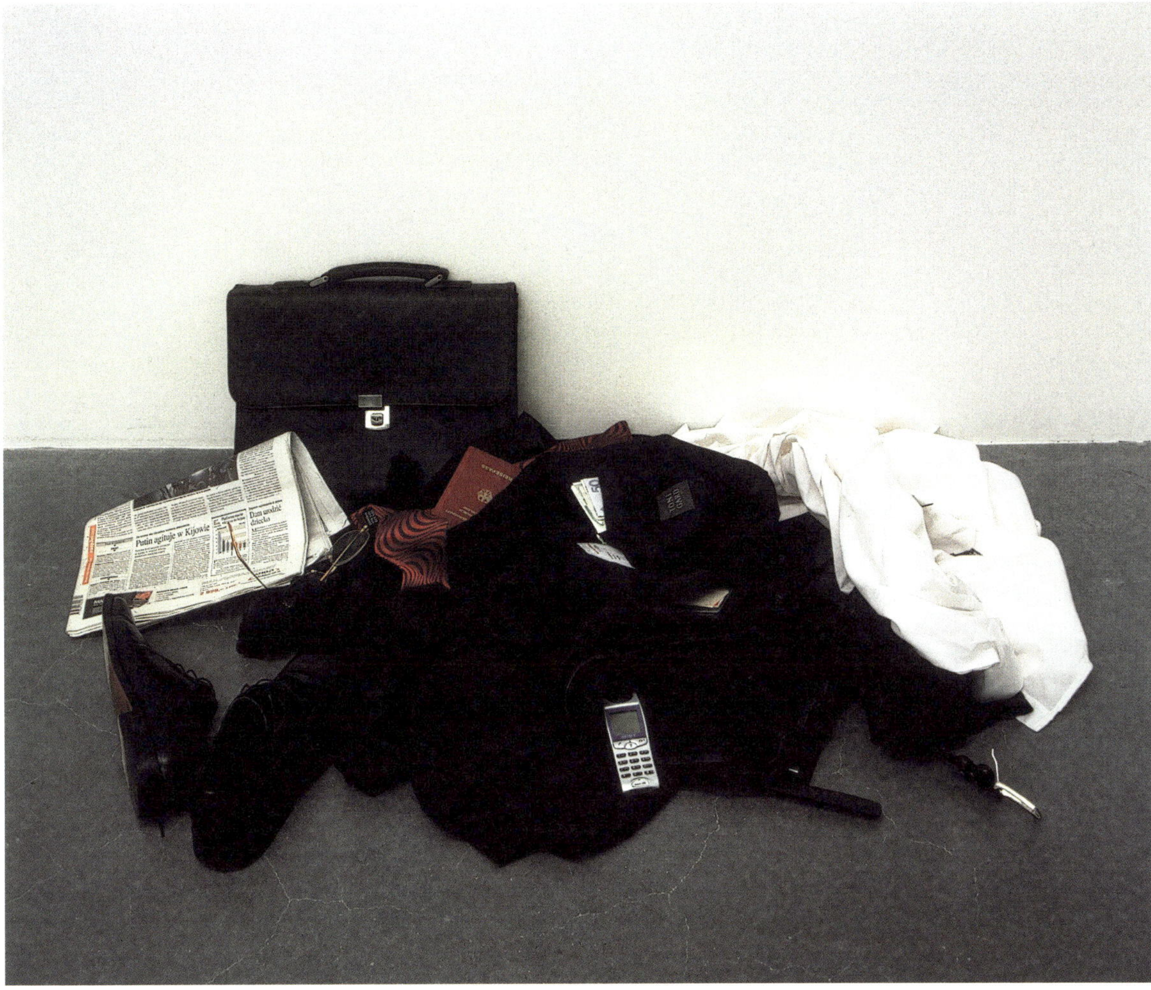

Self-Portrait as a Businessman 2002–4
Installation: leather, textiles, plastic, glass and paper
Tate, purchased with funds provided by the 2004 Outset Frieze Acquisitions Fund for Tate 2004

Following page:
Film 2000–2007
Tate

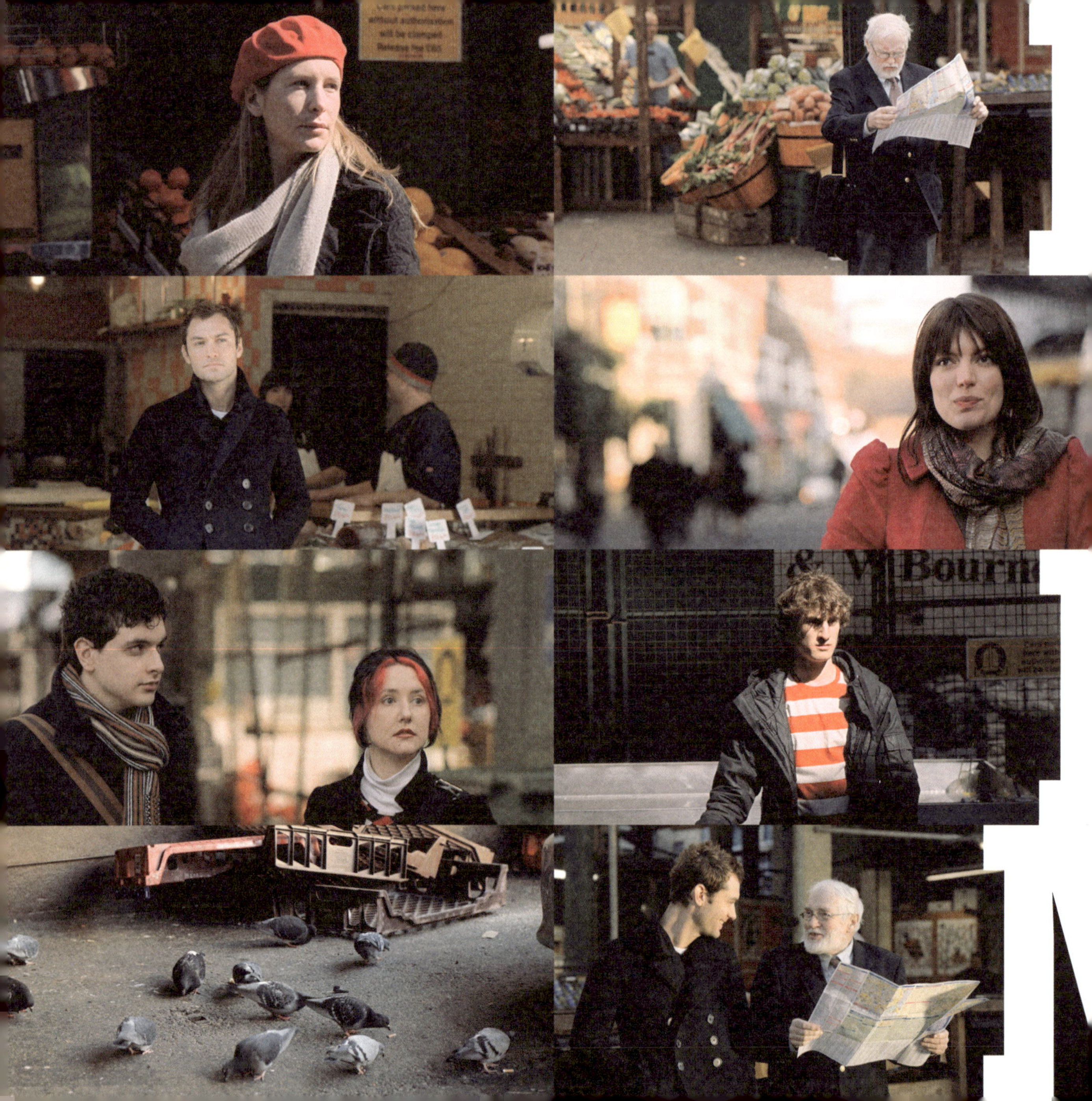

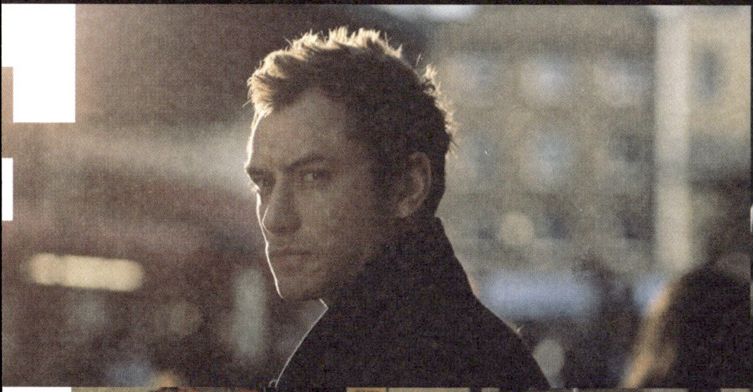
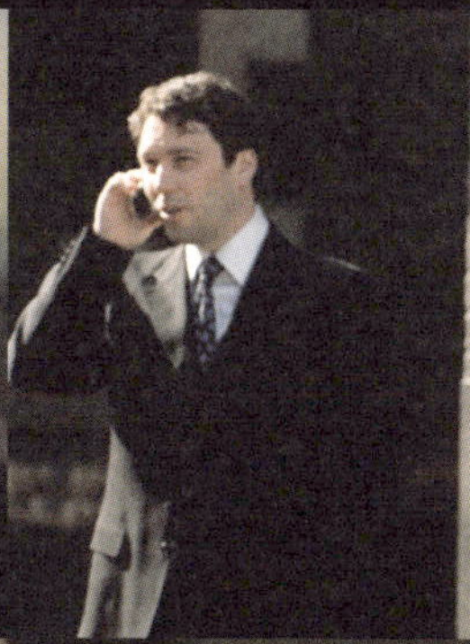
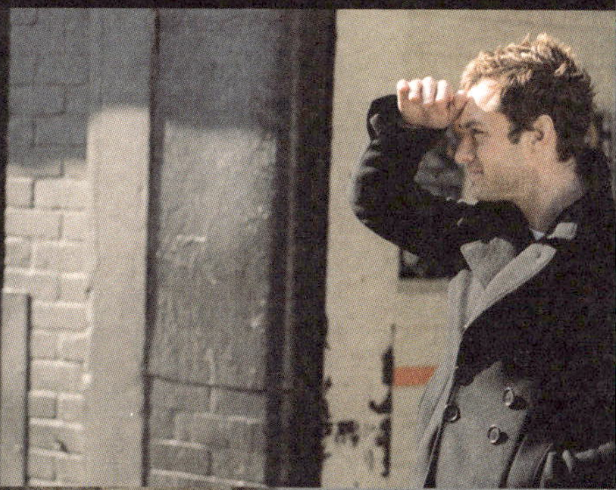
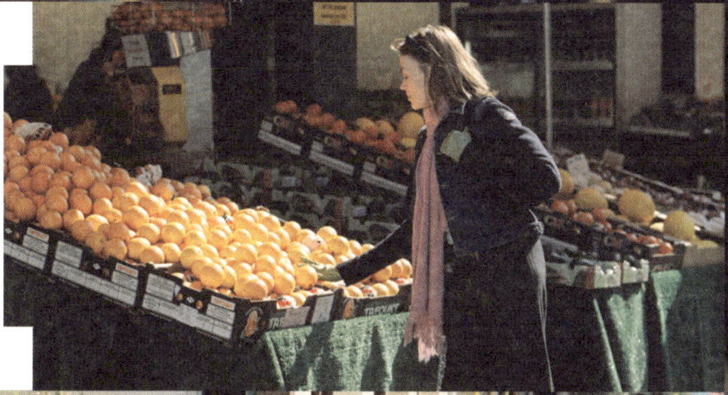
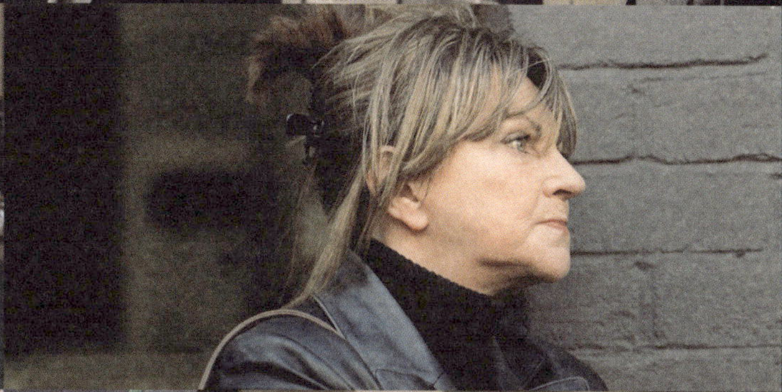
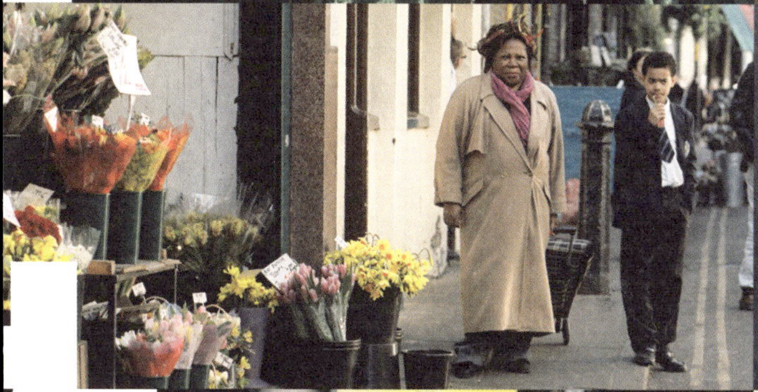
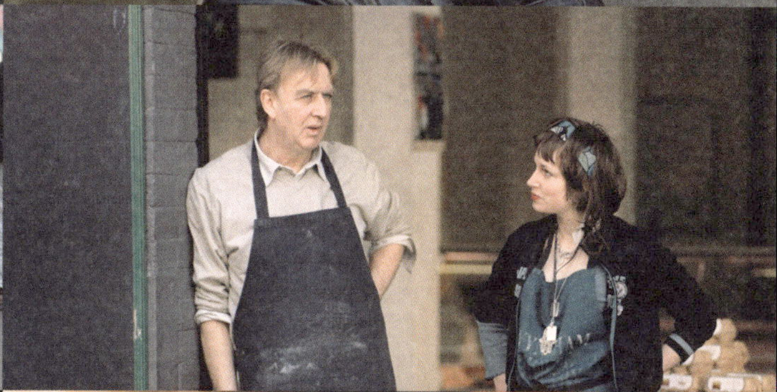
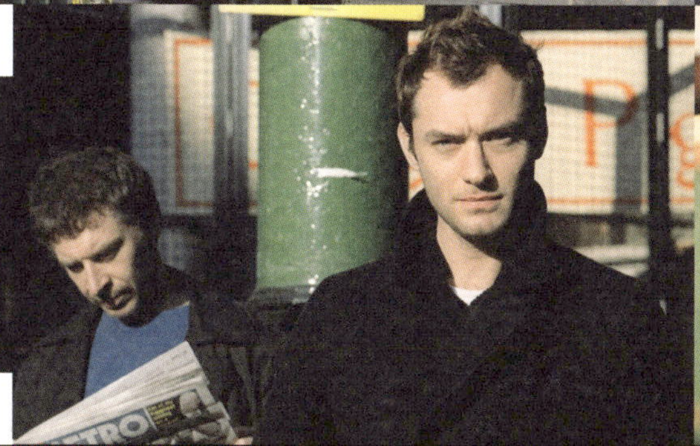
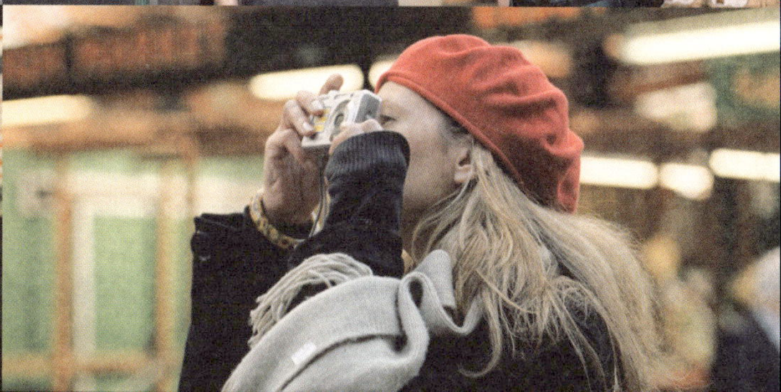

CEZARY BODZIANOWSKI

Delving into the mundane and absurd of the everyday, Cezary Bodzianowski's performances are interventions into habitual situations that catch the passer-by or viewer unaware. These 'moments of life' combine the seemingly random nature of the Surrealist and Dadaist traditions with the sense of humour found in hidden-camera practical jokes. Where possible, Bodzianowski responds specifically to the context of a given situation, enabling the resulting performances to function as considered reflections on social situations and locations.

Works such as the video series *2, 3, 4 x Paris* 2005 emphasise the spontaneous and unwitting participation of tourists in micro-collaborations, focusing on their reactions of surprise, confusion or annoyance. In one vignette, Bodzianowski asks people to take his picture in front of the Eiffel tower with a non-functioning toy camera, and in another, he wanders around a flower garden sporting a plastic 'Elizabethan collar' around his neck. For his contribution to the first Tirana Biennale, *Politi* 2001, the artist assumed the role of personal bodyguard to the curator, Giancarlo Politi, following him everywhere during the opening events. The title is a pun referring both to the curator and to the police (in Danish) This and other performances are documented through photographs and video, often in the casual style of the snapshot or home movie.

Bodzianowski's interventions also involve private or domestic space. In *Good Morning* 1997, he persuaded a crane operator to lift him up to the fifth floor windows of a tower block so that he could wish startled residents a good morning. For *Nattahnam* 1996, he lived with a family of complete strangers for sixteen hours, integrating himself in their daily activities and meals. *Living Room* 2006, a gallery-based installation, consists of a video image of an unpopulated living room projected onto a large curtain. The image appears mostly still, with the exception of the projected curtain, which subtly shifts and twitches as if concealing an intruder. Reminiscent of René Magritte's paintings of domestic interiors, the *unheimlich* (literally 'un-homely', but translated as 'uncanny') is invoked in the unexpected moments of these domestic scenes.

For *World as a Stage*, Bodzianowski exhibits two works. The video *Luna* 2005 features the artist at a children's park inside a large rotating drum. Wearing a pair of rollerblades – one on his foot, the other on his hand – he awkwardly slides, falls and tumbles while attempting to remain upright. Like the buffoonish antithesis of Leonardo Da Vinci's *Vitruvian Man*, the artist struggles to maintain some sense of equilibrium. *Flying Helmet* 2007 is a new commission, a performance and accompanying documentation, in which Bodzianowski measures the exterior dimensions of the Globe Theatre, the reconstructed Shakespearean open-air theatre adjacent to Tate Modern on the Thames. Wryly commenting on the famous English national symbol, Bodzianowski then measures out relational dimensions on an actual globe, a scale model of the planet Earth. One the one hand, this work is a consideration of the worldliness of the diverse cultures (mis)represented in the Bard's histories, comedies, and tragedies, while on the other, it is an absurdly literal recognition of the discrepancy in scale between two globes. *Cliff Lauson*

Luna (still) 2005
Video
Courtesy Foksal Gallery Foundation, Warsaw

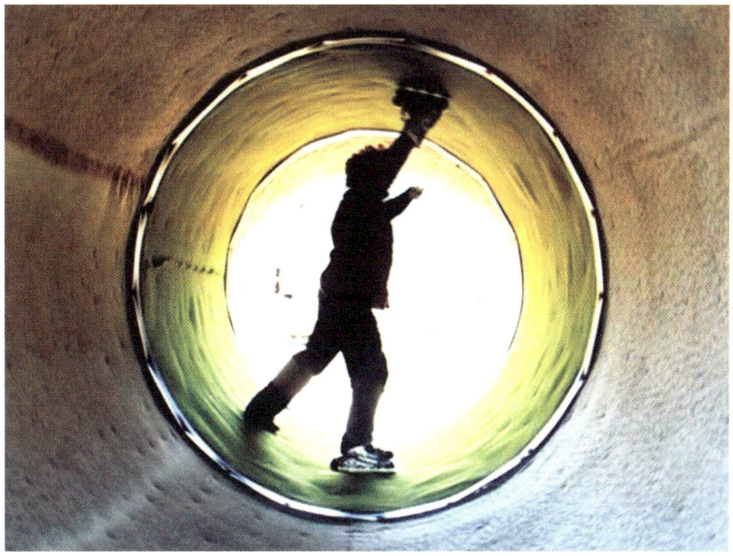

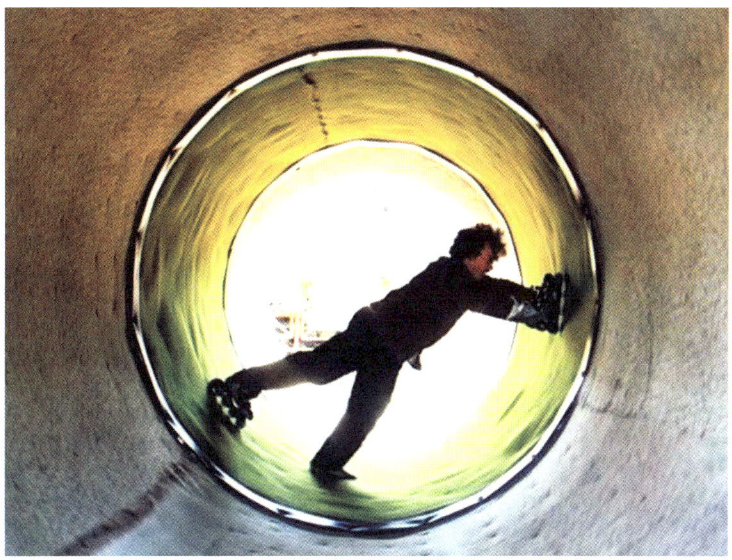

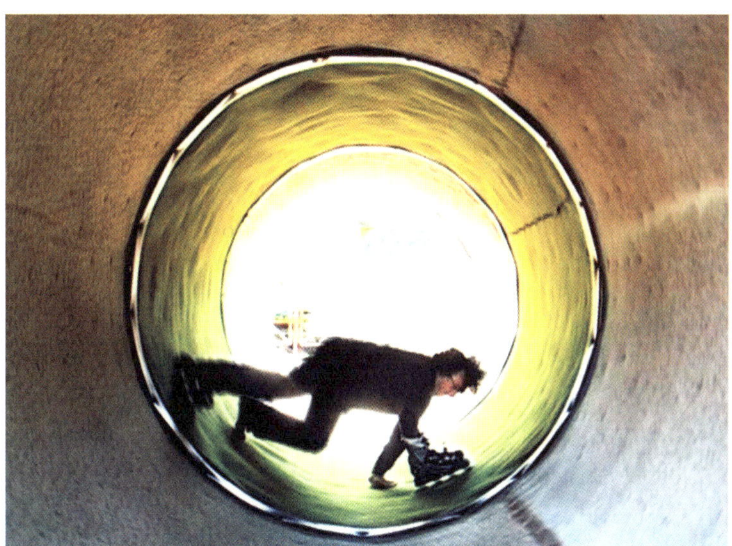

ULLA VON BRANDENBURG

Ulla von Brandenburg's work is inspired by imagery dating from the era at the end of the nineteenth and beginning of the twentieth centuries, a period that saw an increased interest in the paranormal, the dawn of psychoanalysis and the parallel rise of vaudeville and socially aware theatre. All of these elements inform her conceptual strategies. Her practice has explored the occult and the mysteries of the unconscious, drawing on stylised approaches to performance.

Von Brandenburg makes drawings, watercolours, murals, installations and films. The transition between media is often an important component in her work; she highlights the narrative potential of the still image, or, conversely, an iconic singularity in the moving image. Her silhouette drawings and murals are frequently inspired by found photographs. A large untitled work of 2003 is based on Henry Peach Robinson's 1858 photograph of a dying girl in an interior surrounded by grieving relatives. Von Brandenburg's wall mural is realised in a two-tone palette with a simplified, flat composition. A more recent drawing, *Back*, shows a seated man facing away from the viewer. His dapper suit, boater hat and walking stick immediately identify him as a character from another age, while his posture suggests that he is reflecting on an unfathomable past. Von Brandenburg's cool, abstracted style suggests that memory and history are only clear in outline.

Von Brandenburg's *tableau vivant* are like filmic friezes. Shot on super 8mm or 16mm film, they depict stylised groupings of figures. Her sitters remain as still as possible, attempting to hold their static poses for the duration of the films. Their costumes and positioning encourage the viewer to read relationships between the figures and imagine stories to explain their configurations. In *Key* 2007, ten young men and women in contemporary dress are depicted in a dark interior. They all appear to be engaged in moments of introspection or occupied by private rituals: two women exchange a key while in another part of the composition a man gestures towards a ribbon-draped sofa. The *tableau* re-imagines old source material and antiquated forms of representation, suggesting a chronological rift between the slow, ambiguous time alluded to in the films and the present real time in which they are shown.

Taking the form of the *tableau vivant* a little further, *Around* 2005 is a silent film in which a tightly packed group of figures stand with their backs to the camera in the middle of a street. As the camera travels around them, the figures shift their position so that no frontal aspect is ever revealed. The minimal choreography of the figures' shuffling movement puts the viewer in the position of voyeuristic outsider. The cyclical and repetitive nature of the film emphasises a sense of deferral and ambiguity.

Von Brandenburg has made two works for *The World as Stage*. In a new film, her characters are seen reflected in a mirrored ball in a garden setting. The reflective surface allows the viewer to see the artist and her camera, heightening the constructed artifice of the scene. The other work is a reconstruction of the patchwork curtain designed in 1932 by Walpole Champneys for the Royal Shakespeare Theatre in Stratford-upon-Avon. Von Brandenburg has remade the curtain in different colours. The slight gap where the curtains meet in the middle implies a world that is screened off behind it and as such the viewer's position is made unclear; we are simultaneously actors and audience in some unspecified performance. *Rachel Taylor*

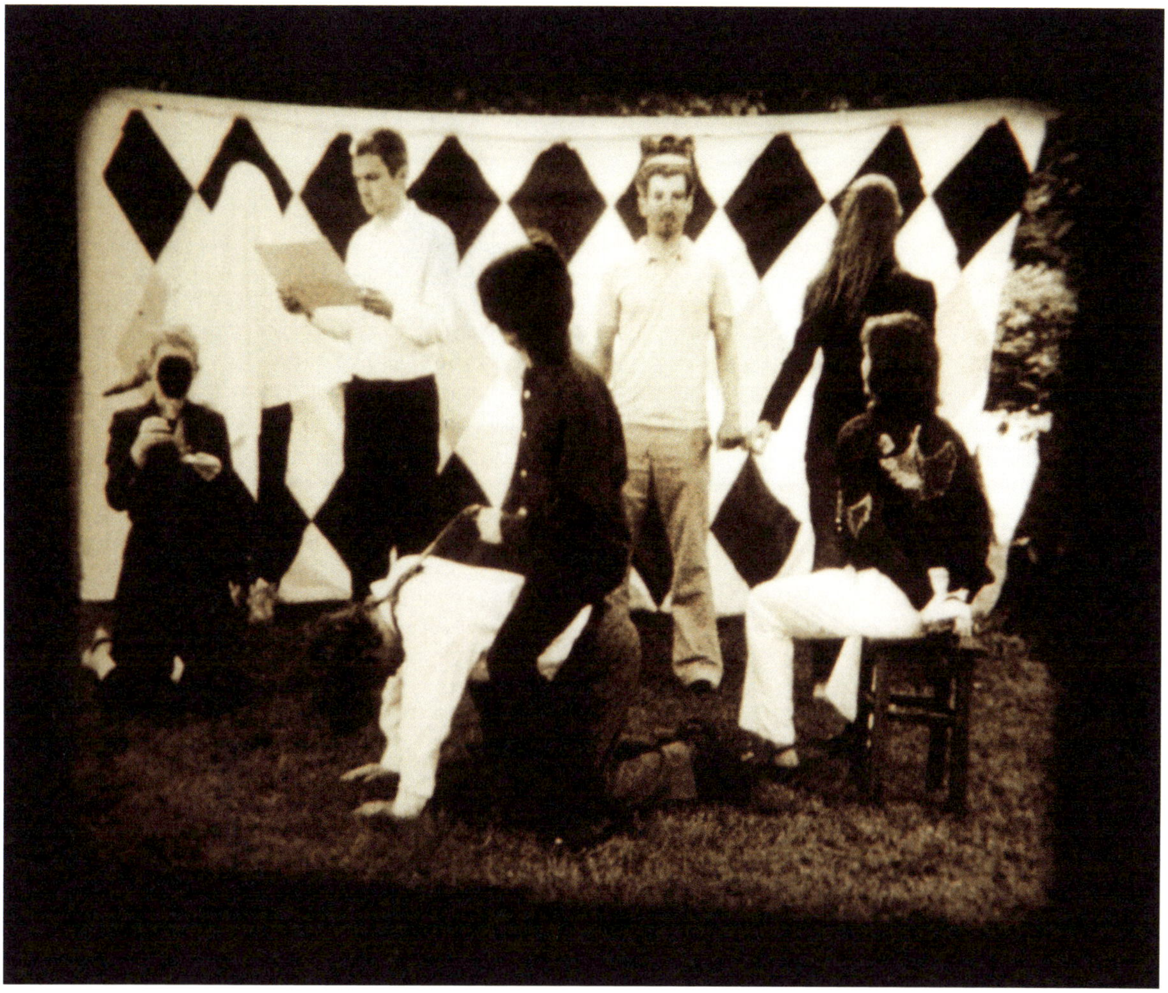

Reiter 2004
Super 8mm film, black and white, silent
Courtesy of the artist and Produzentengalerie, Hamburg

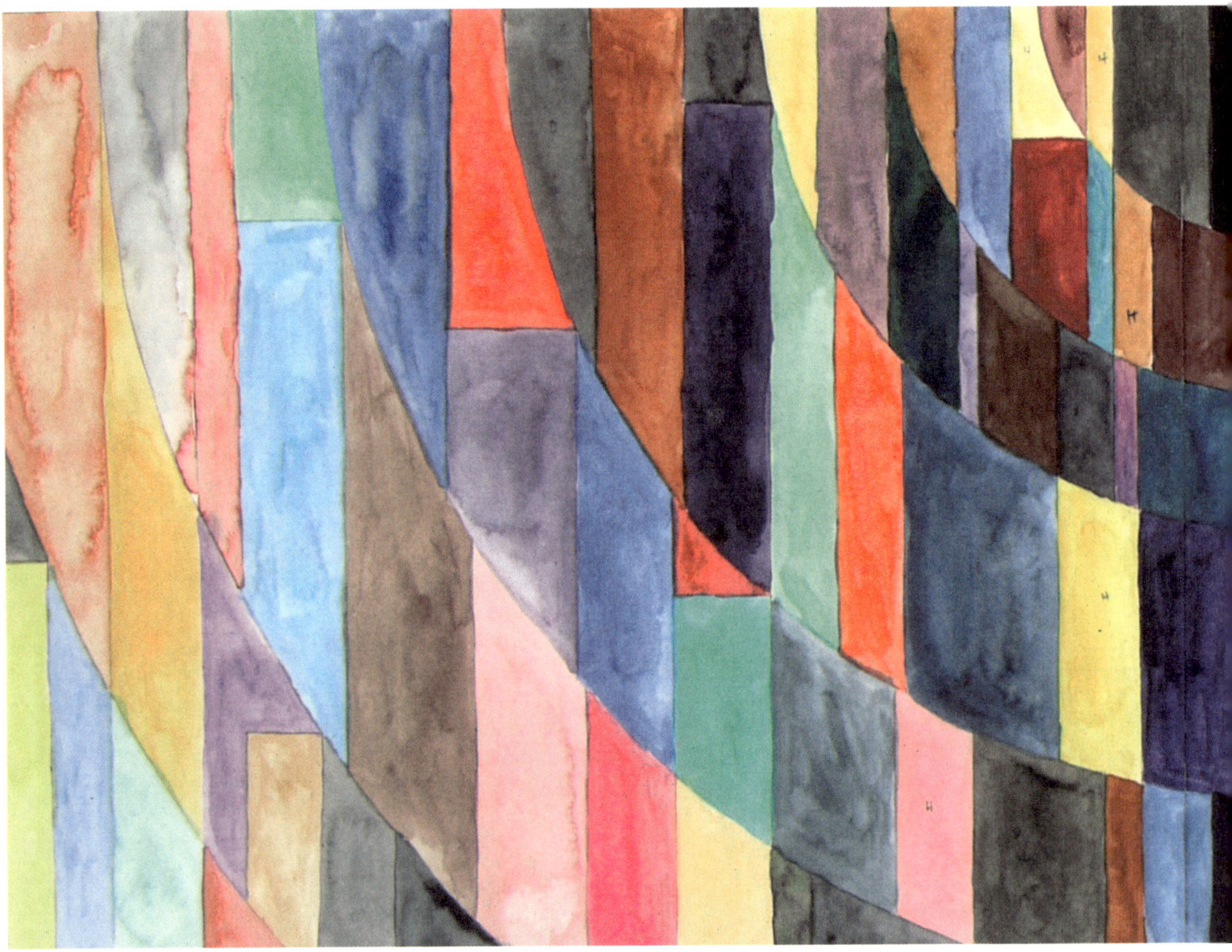

Curtain 2007
Watercolour on paper
Courtesy of the artist and Produzentengalerie, Hamburg

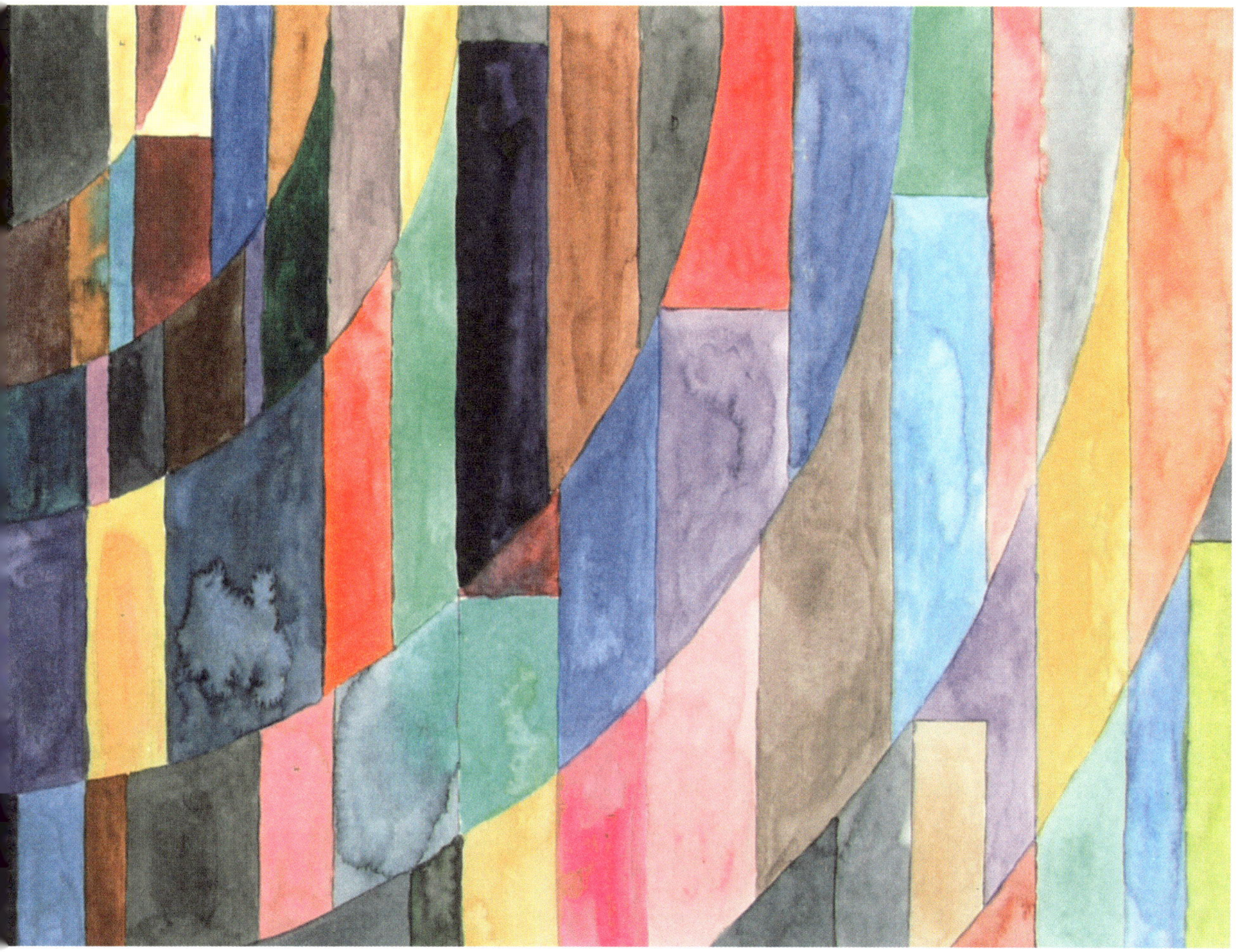

JEREMY DELLER

In Jeremy Deller's work we find a potent collision of contradictions: often, a celebratory and light-hearted framework is undercut by dark currents of raw emotion. 'A sense of reality keeps breaking into the evident theatre of it',[1] writes Tom Lubbock in his description of *The Battle of Orgreave* 2002. In this work, Deller stages a re-enactment of the violent clash between police and picket line at the Orgreave coking plant in South Yorkshire on 18 June 1984. He invited former miners and policemen who were involved in the original battle to participate alongside members of battle re-enactment societies from all over the United Kingdom. Both Deller and Artangel, the commissioning body, were aware of the sensitivity of restaging the event and its potential to escalate out of control. Michael Morris, Co-Director of Artangel, describes it in retrospect: 'We gave ourselves a year in which to build bridges of trust with the community of former miners in South Yorkshire and resolved to abandon the project at the first sign of hostility.'[2] Deller states: 'I would never have undertaken the project if people locally felt it was unnecessary or in poor taste. As it was, we encountered a lot of support from the outset because there seemed to be an instinctive understanding of what the re-enactment was about.'[3] Much of the film focuses on the careful preparations that were made for the re-enactment, the result of over a year of extensive research by Deller spent in archives reading, listening and interviewing many of those involved. A question emerges regarding the extent to which the original battle was planned and orchestrated by the government and police rather than being provoked by the violent behaviour of the picketers. Tony Benn, MP, describes how the BBC coverage of the event was edited to make the miners appear to have started the violence, a misrepresentation for which the BBC was subsequently forced to apologise. Deller therefore demonstrates how the line between truth and reality is blurred not just in the re-enactment but also in the original event. He states: 'As an artist I was interested in how far an idea could be taken, especially an idea that is on the face of it a contradiction in terms "a recreation of something that was essentially chaos".'[4]

Much of Deller's work involves collaboration with individuals and often focuses on community events or performances. *Folk Archive* 2005, a collaboration with Alan Kane, presents a very personal and eclectic selection of objects, drawings, documentation of events and even websites that Deller and Kane feel reflect contemporary popular art in the UK. The collection includes documentary footage of bizarre English events such as Egremont Crab Fair in Cumbria, established in 1387, which involves a Pipe Smoking Competition, Wheelbarrow Racing and The World Gurning Championships. *Folk Archive* also includes, among many other curiosities, a selection of hand-stitched trade-union and activist banners, drawings by prisoners, photos of crop circles, novelty cakes, and tea cosies. As in much of Deller's work, we see in *Folk Archive* a celebration of the creativity of diverse and vibrant communities rarely showcased within art institutions and galleries. His projects delve deep into the social and political fabric of our society, often providing an opportunity to re-examine and to represent ourselves. *Maeve Polkinhorn*

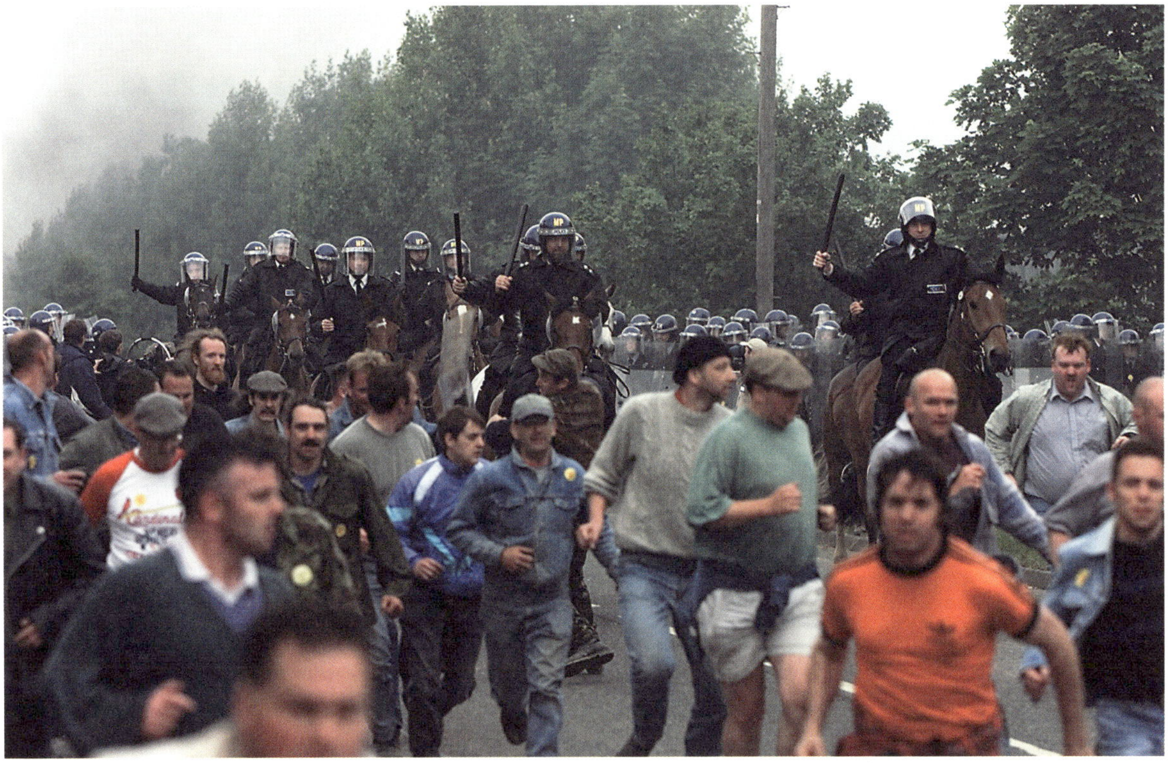

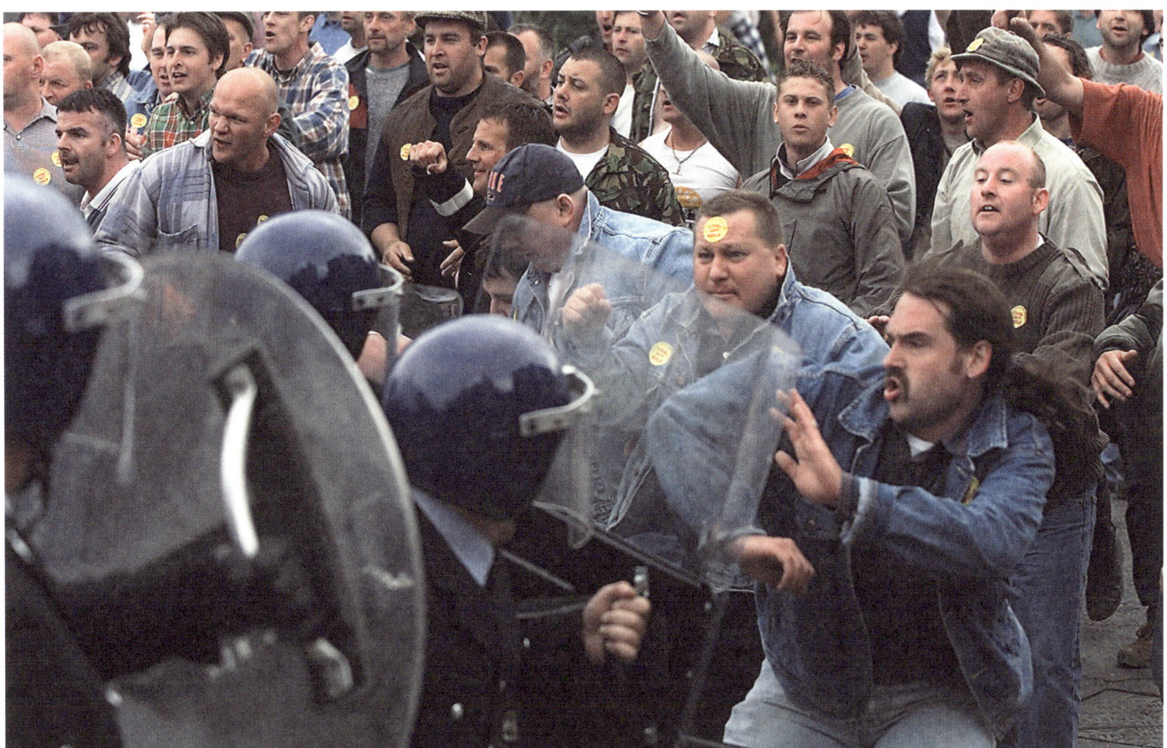

The Battle of Orgreave (still) 2001
Film
Commissioned and produced by Artangel
Tate

TRISHA DONNELLY

Trisha Donnelly's diverse practice reflects and illustrates the boundaries of the fathomable. Her work explores the disjunction between recognition and comprehension, an intellectual and psychological terrain in which things lose their way, get displaced, bump up against and fracture into other thoughts, memories and allusions. This theoretical no man's land is the breeding ground of interdisciplinarity (think of the synaesthetic experiments of artists from Kandinsky to Nabokov) and free association (Freud's parsing of the mind's labyrinthine syntax).

An early photograph, *Blind Friends* 2001, provides a visual metaphor for Donnelly's fractal-like approach. The photograph depicts a group of lost-looking people wandering on a beach. The artist gathered the group and asked them to walk in the direction of the wind, but the photograph records each person choosing a different direction. Here a seemingly simple task is complicated by the subjective and individual vagaries of perception and interpretation.

Donnelly reflects and illustrates the often indescribable moments when we experience a shock of recognition of the infinite. These experiences induce transport or rapture, not in a spiritual sense but closer to the epiphanies of scientific discovery. Because this is the territory of revelation and the unknown, her work has often been contextualised in terms of acts of belief, but her interest is in the metaphysical rather than the mystical.

Her practice has consistently played with notions of performance. A recent facet of her work is the illustrated lecture, in which she combines allusive images with theoretical musings on a variety of topics, from sixteenth-century Russian history to prismatic vision. She has also staged 'demonstrations' to mark the opening of her exhibitions. These demonstrations are never documented; they exist only as memories and stories passed on by those who witnessed them. At the opening of her 2004 show at Casey Kaplan Gallery, she played a piece of music, then led a procession through New York's Chelsea to the Wrong Gallery, behind whose doorway the deafening noise of a cannon resounded. The music and the cannon fire were audio signifiers of the beginning and end of a wormhole, a hypothetical shortcut through the space-time continuum. The period between these two audio pieces represented a heightened moment for the assembled crowd during which they surrendered ordinary notions of time.

Donnelly has also used a sound, which cannot be transcribed into words, to title a group of drawings. Another series of text-based works feature words with the vowels removed. *The Passenger* is reduced to 'tH.PSNGR' and 'berserk' to 'BZRK'.These truncations recall the stuttering syntax of text messages and scientific abbreviations.

The Redwood and the Raven addresses issues of continuity and memory, and presents an interdisciplinary mingling of photography, poetry and dance. The work consists of thirty-one photographs of the modern dancer Frances Flannery in front of a redwood tree performing a dance she choreographed to Edgar Allan Poe's poem 'The Raven'. Each image in the series is shown individually during the exhibition so that the dancer's performance is gradually revealed over the course of time, the choreography becoming apparent only by repeated visits to the gallery. Donnelly subjects the dancer's actions to extension and compression, simultaneously accentuating the flattening of Flannery's body into two-dimensional shapes and highlighting the temporal potential of the photographic image. *Rachel Taylor*

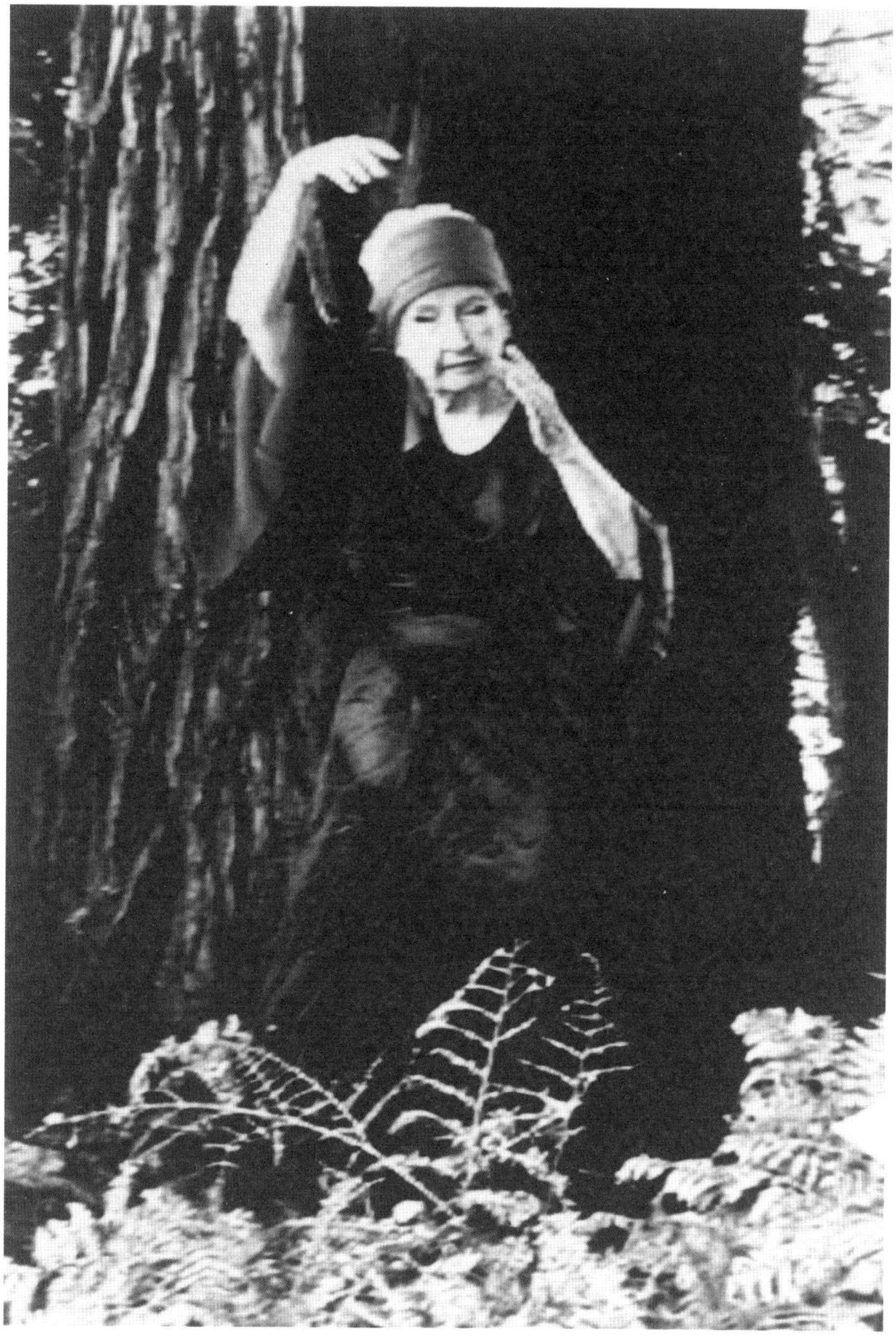

The Redwood and the Raven (detail) 2004
Thirty-one black and white photographs on paper
Tate, purchased with funds provided by the 2006
Outset Frieze Acquisitions Fund for Tate 2007

GEOFFREY FARMER

Geoffrey Farmer's research-based practice is broad-ranging and verges on the obsessive. Often site-specific and performative, his work consists of accumulations of material related to a given subject, typically drawing on images and narratives from popular culture and literature. He frequently transforms his installations over the course of his exhibitions by making interventions in the gallery space while it is closed to the public. This may involve adding or removing components, or making videos of private performances in the space, which are then incorporated into the works.

Every surface in some way decorated, altered, or changed forever (except the float) 2004 at the Catriona Jeffries Gallery in Vancouver was a large sculptural installation based on a parade float. During the course of the project a wooden float structure was constructed in the centre of the space. Costumes, drawings, texts and decorations were made and gradually introduced, eventually burying the float structure and making the gallery impossible to enter. More recently, Farmer created a similarly metamorphic work, *Airliner Open Studio* 2006, using a section of a commercial airplane, formerly used as a film set, as his visual centrepiece and conceptual starting point. Over the course of the exhibition, he explored the set after hours, documenting his interactions on video and presenting these daily along with his sculptural interventions and drawings. Farmer's light-hearted and spontaneous approach emphasises experimentation and highlights the backstage workings of artistic production and the darkened gallery after closing.

The interactive and transformative tendencies of Farmer's work were perhaps most dramatically realised in *A Pale Fire Freedom Machine* 2005 at the Power Plant in Toronto. This installation included carefully arranged rows of found wooden furniture including desks, bookshelves and chairs surrounding a rotating steel fireplace. Over the course of the exhibition, gallery assistants dismantled the furniture and fed it into the fireplace. The resulting ash was used to produce a text work and an abstract print that visitors could take away.

Farmer's interest in staging and performance is evident in *Room 302* 2005, made in collaboration with Judy Radul. The work consists of video documentation of a sound recording of actors reading from transcripts of real and fictional trials. The actors are located in a once real courtroom that now functions as a set for television and film productions. The video is projected onto the dismantled facade of the courtroom set. The sculptural component of the work shares the scatter aesthetic of Farmer's previous work, apparently haphazard yet deliberately placed. The video element, a literal courtroom drama, explicitly engages with the theatrical. The restaged trial scenes conflate and confuse the performative aspect of the legal process with its dramatic reconstruction.

Farmer's contribution to *The World as a Stage* is his multi-media installation *Hunchback Kit* 2000–07. The kit, which comprises a group of found and constructed objects, props, photographs and texts contained within an eleven foot travelling crate, is conceived as a continual adaptation and interpretation of Victor Hugo's 1831–2 novel *Notre-Dame de Paris*. Although some of the objects in the kit can be read as props or costumes relating to various characters in the novel, Farmer's work alludes to broader philosophical questions embedded in Hugo's narrative and its subsequent readings. The installation has no set display parameters, but is accompanied by a manual that suggests possible configurations of the disparate components. In essence a new work is produced each time the kit is shown. Reflecting his adaptable methodology, Farmer encourages a flexible approach in the presentation of *Hunchback Kit* that echoes its open-ended allusions. *Rachel Taylor*

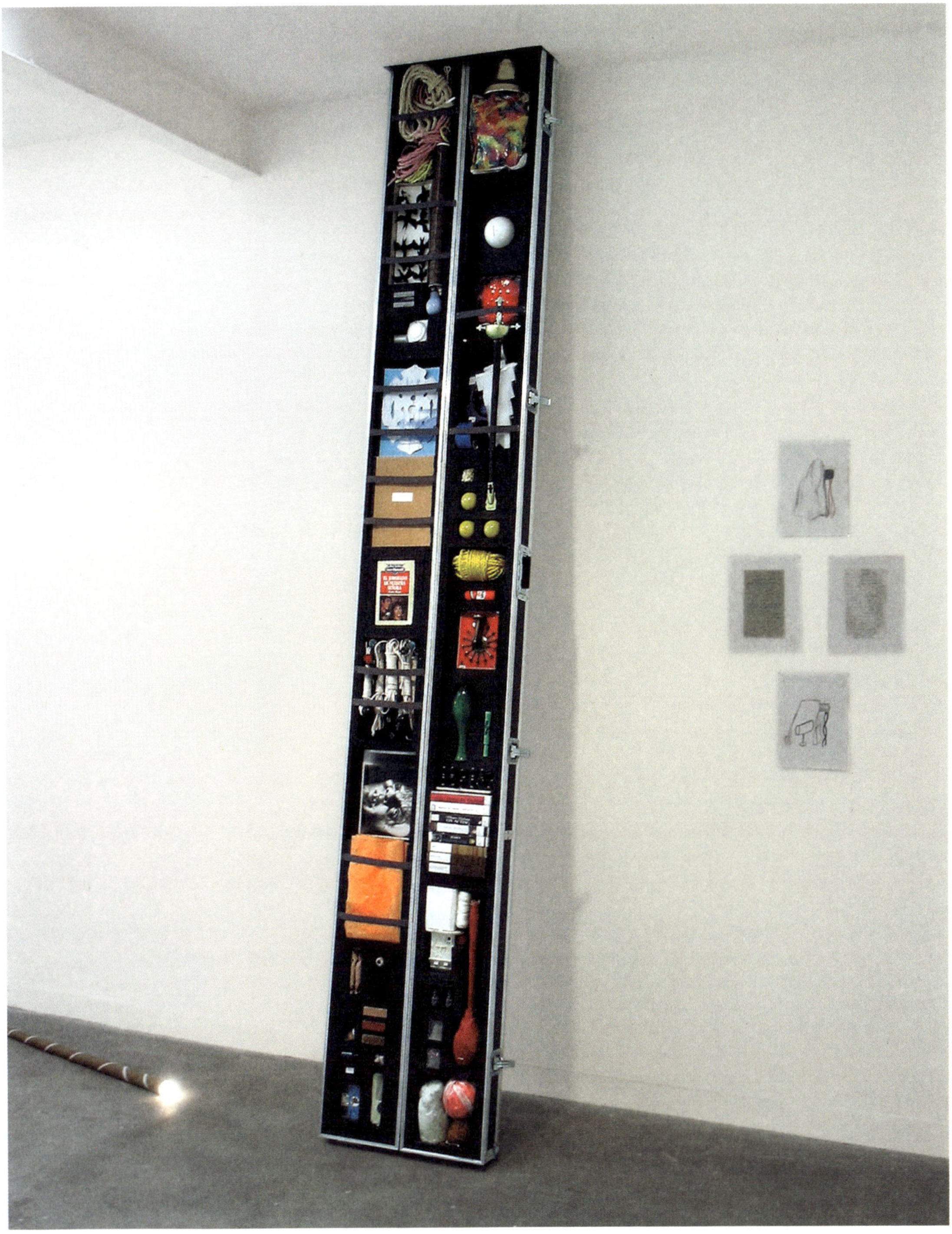

Hunchback Kit 2000
Mixed media
Installation view, Gasworks Gallery 2002
Collection of the Vancouver Art Gallery, Vancouver Art Gallery Acquisition Fund and purchased with the financial support of the Canada Council for the Arts Acquisitions Assistance program
Courtesy Catriona Jeffries Gallery, Vancouver

Following page:
A Pale Fire Freedom Machine 2005
Installation view, The Power Plant, Toronto
Rennie Collection, Vancouver
Courtesy Catriona Jeffries Gallery, Vancouver

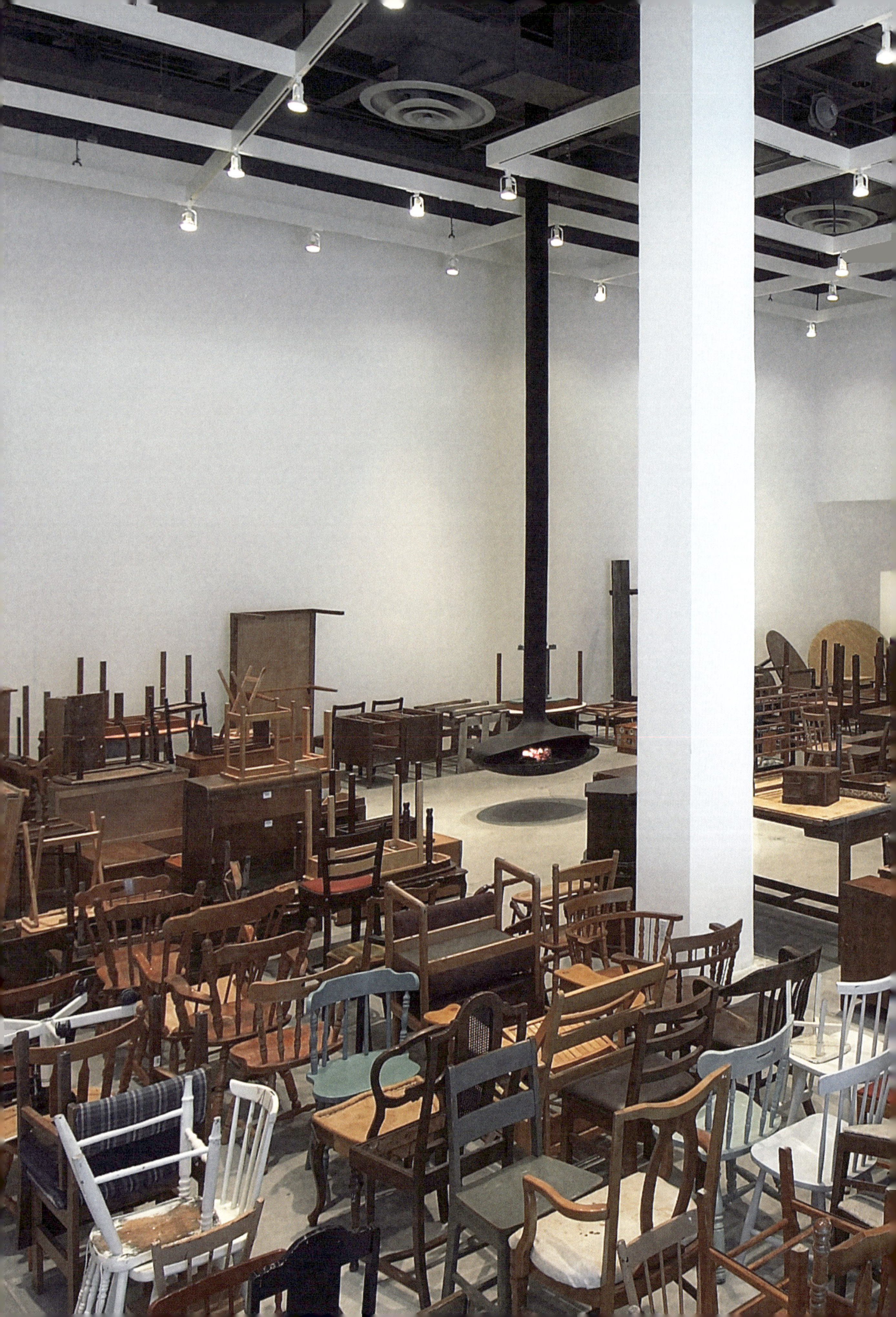

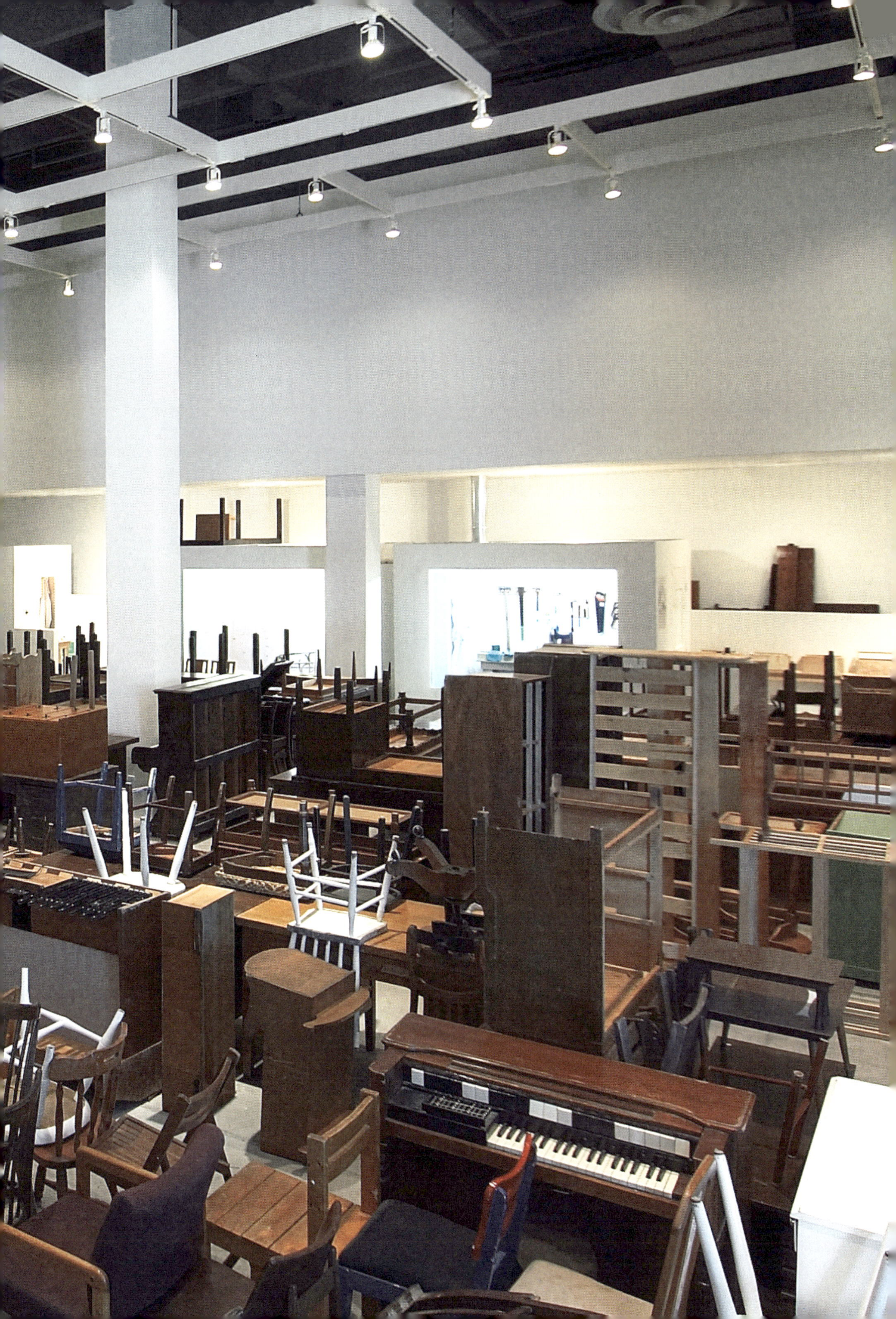

ANDREA FRASER

With dry humour, Andrea Fraser's work critically analyses the forms of presentation, hierarchies and methods of exclusion that operate within art institutions and the art world in general. In a number of works, she appropriates the museum's tools of interpretation and publicity – the gallery talk, wall text, museum poster and audioguide – in order to create her own satirical versions, which expose and critique the ways in which artists, viewers and art objects are staged and manipulated.

Little Frank and his Carp 2001 was inspired by the text of the Guggenheim Bilbao's audioguide, which Fraser sees 'as a particularly outrageous example of the way corporatized museums … are packaging artistic transgression and transcendence, subversion and sensuality'.[1] In this video work, we see an unauthorised performance by Fraser, shot via hidden camera, taking place in the atrium of Frank Gehry's building in Bilbao. She obediently responds to the script of the audioguide, which advocates, among other things, sensuously stroking the museum walls. In *A Visit to the Sistine Chapel* 2005, again we see Fraser dutifully obeying the audioguide's recommendations, but this time in the context of the Vatican. She is told to be a pious visitor. This becomes a difficult task as Fraser is herded along with other tourists through the Vatican's rooms. The artworks' religious and meditative qualities are lost in the highly commercial and mediated mass-tourism experience that a visit to the Vatican has become.

In *Museum Highlights: A Gallery Talk* 1989, we see the artist acting the role of a volunteer museum guide, Jane Castleton, at the Philadelphia Museum of Art. Following extensive research, Fraser constructed a script for Castleton, whom she conceived 'not as a character but as a site defined by her function as the museum's representative'.[2] The script is composed as a cacophony of quotes from a wide range of archival sources, including the *Philadelphia Museum of Art Handbook* (1931), Octavia Hill's *Good Housing that Pays* (1917) and Immanuel Kant's *Critique of Judgement* (1790). It juxtaposes nineteenth-century descriptions of poorhouses with those of the museum, linking the two institutions as instruments of methods of urban social control, each with their systems of incentives and disincentives, goads and deterrents.

Fraser states about her work: 'I'm happy to identify myself with Institutional Critique, but "institutional analysis" may be even better … You could say that all my work is about the repressed fantasies of our field and about the desires produced and pursued through these fantasies.'[3] In *Museum Highlights*, Castleton's exaggerations and enthusiasms often become ridiculous and irrational, such as when she eulogises over a drinking fountain, describing it as 'a work of astonishing economy and monumentality'. Despite their rigorous research and analytic artistic strategy, Fraser's works are often also extremely funny, achieving 'a kind of irrational result in the very excess of its rationalization'.[4] *Maeve Polkinhorn*

Opposite page, top to bottom:
Museum Highlights: A Gallery Talk 1989
A Visit to the Sistine Chapel 2005
Little Frank and His Carp 2001
All: video
Courtesy the artist and Friedrich Petzel Gallery, New York

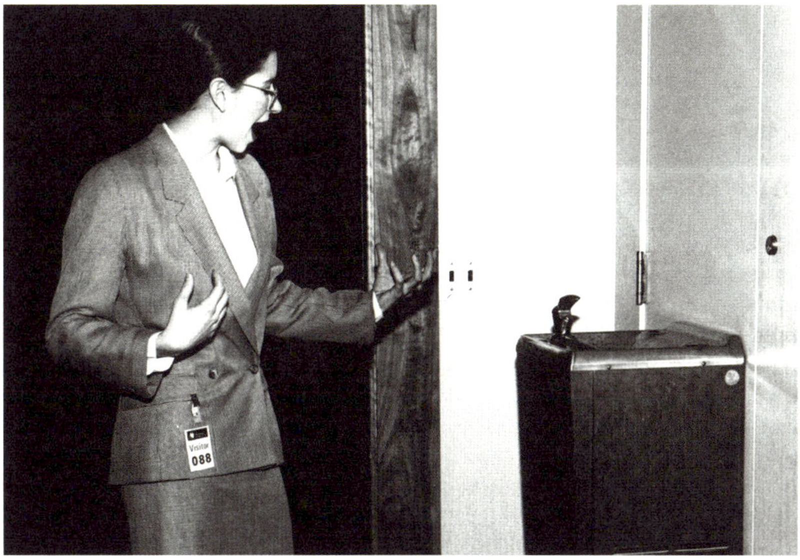
Visitor
088

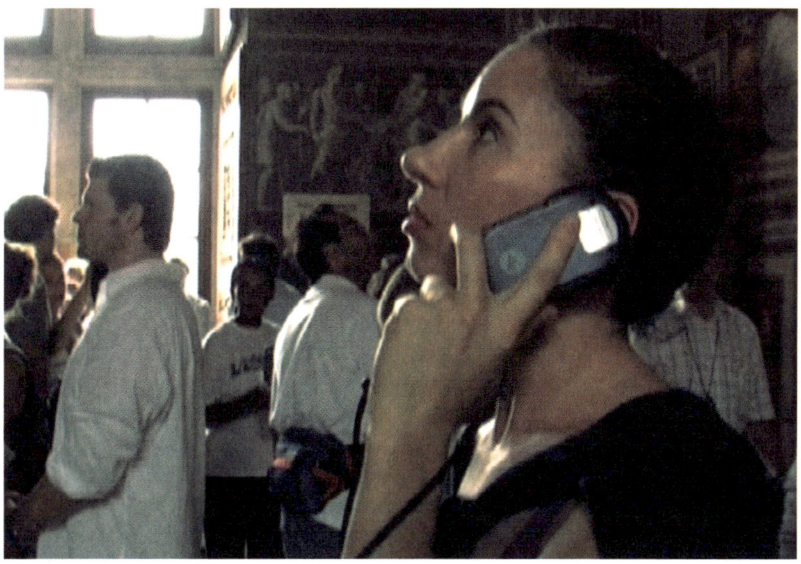

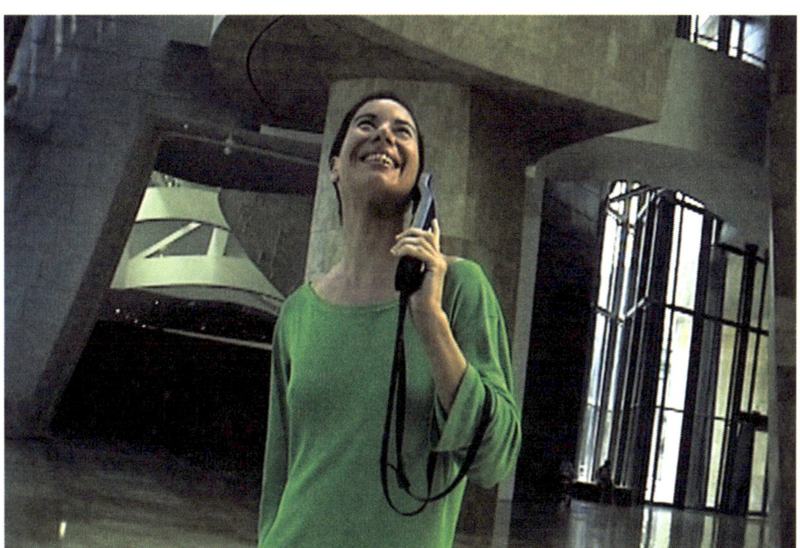

DOMINIQUE GONZALEZ-FOERSTER

Dominique Gonzalez-Foerster works across a multiplicity of media and contexts, intentionally blurring the meeting point between visual art and other fields of cultural production, such as design and architecture, in the process of searching for new forms. The perception of time and space are the common denominators that inform her practice. Whether in her gallery environments, films or interventions outdoors, subjective experience and the way in which its related physical sensations and emotions are translated into visual form always come into question.

Séance de Shadow II 1998 bathes an empty room in a deep blue atmosphere. This is a passage where visitors can circulate, moving from one space to the next. By entering the room, however, viewers realise that their presence is triggering a cinematic theatre of shadows. The work is a living surface onto which is cast the evanescent shadows of bodies and objects, registering their passing through the space. A real-time performance is created, in which the visitors become the actors.

Park – A Plan to Escape 2002 was an installation that took the visitors on a journey through a park in Kassel, Germany. Gonzalez-Foerster used the garden as the site for a new environment: a world of unique objects such as a palm tree, a piece of architecture, a street lamp, a chair, a large stone, a phone booth, all related to personal moments that seemed to define a fragmented script. The idea developed in a series of works made throughout the 1990s that consisted of designed interiors such as *The Moriya Room* 1994 and *Une chambre en ville* 1996. These reconstitutions of intimate places were carefully lit *mises-en-scène* of objects and furniture, staging Gonzalez-Foerster's attempt to revive her own memory of places, films, novels, and lived moments, emptied of any human presence. They neverthless invited viewers to project their own thoughts and physical connections onto the surroundings. As Gonzalez-Foerster stated: 'The position of the viewer is a constantly evolving one, sometimes disturbed by unconscious choreographies.'[1]

Gonzalez-Foester's films carry out a similar exploration into the physical experience of places and time, particularly the sensations provided by the discovery of new places. The filmic medium lends itself well to the depiction of an atmosphere and of a transitional experience while embracing the vocabulary of contemporary media culture. If Gonzalez-Foerster's films always involve the presence of a narrator, without whom stories cannot be told, landscapes are the protagonists of her eerie scenarios. Films such as *Riyo* 1999, *Central* 2001 or *Plages* 2001 depict the artist's experience of those places, and capture a feeling of renewed but fragmentary perception. In these films, the position of the artist is that of the *flâneur*, melancholically observing the rhythm of modern life as a distant spectacle.

One of Gonzalez-Foerster's recent installations, *Promenade* 2007,[2] led the viewer through the empty curved gallery of the Musée d'Art Moderne de la Ville de Paris, immersed in the sound of tropical rainfall. This work highlighted one of the most essential elements in Gonzalez-Foerster's projects: the recreation of a once-experienced atmosphere, a cartography of sensations revived through the evocative potential of objects, images, lights and sound. *Vanessa Desclaux*

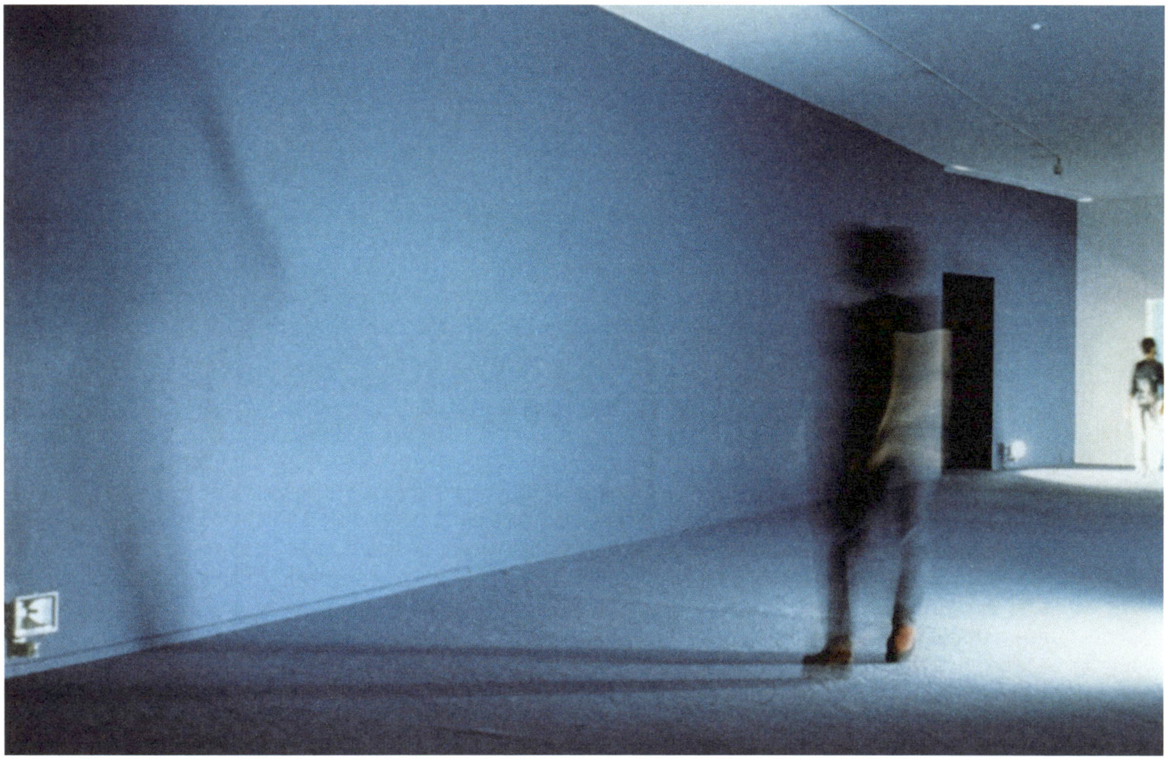

Séance de Shadow II (bleu) 1998
Installation view at Musée d'Art Moderne de la Ville de Paris 1998
Courtesy Esther Schipper, Berlin

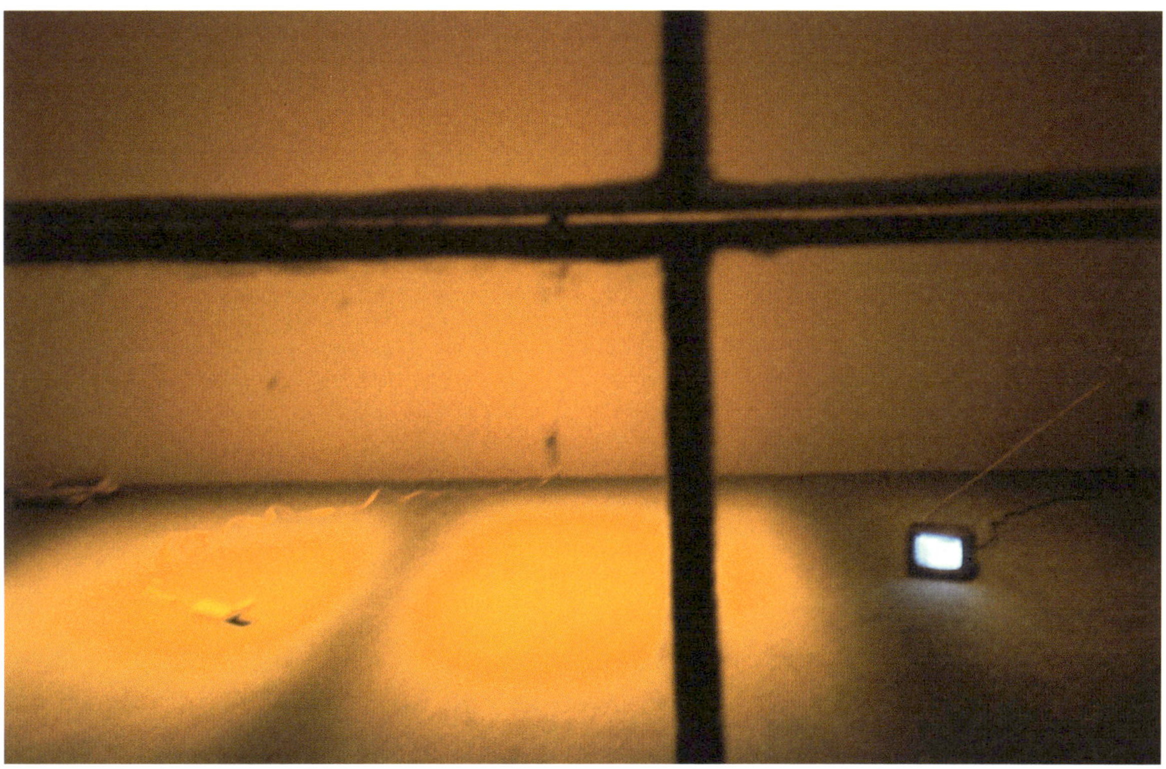

Une chambre en ville 1996
Installation view at Galerie Mot & Van den Boogaard, Brussels
Courtesy Jan Mot, Brussels

JEPPE HEIN

Jeppe Hein's work highlights the interplay between the work, its viewers and the space, emphasising the interdependence of these three elements to create meaning. He 'stage-manages' the viewer such that, willingly or not, he or she becomes a protagonist within the work. Whether it is the triggering of a smoke machine, for *Smoking Bench* 2003, or the sudden appearance of a wall of water as in *Space in Action / Action in Space* 2002 and *Appearing Rooms* 2004, the viewer is surprised or shocked into a physical and vocal reaction – strikingly so, for example, when the china plate of *Please do not touch the Artwork* 2003 falls off the gallery wall and shatters. Much of his work playfully provokes a mixture of pleasure and anxiety, curiosity and fear. Our physical and emotional experience and reaction to the work are integral to it, so that we become both subject and object. Hein therefore disturbs and critiques our expectations of the artwork and the art institution as static, didactic and solemn, and of the visitor as silent, passive and contemplative.

Hein's work builds upon the shift away from the object to experiments in dance, performance, film and video that were undertaken in the 1960s and 1970s by artists as diverse as Robert Morris, Bruce Nauman, Hélio Oiticica, Lygia Clark, Sol LeWitt and Robert Smithson. He shares with these practices the adoption of experimental open systems and rules that involve the viewer and serve to define and generate the art, in particular utilising the form of the cube and/or labyrinths. However, Hein's work differs from these process-based works of 1960s and 1970s in that it embraces the culture of the spectacle and frequently requires some ingenious technical element that is concealed from view in order to produce these spectacular results. A corner of *Burning Cube* 2005, for example, literally catches fire in front of the viewer within the gallery. As Barbara Steiner points out, Hein's work is characterised in all respects by a 'double bind': 'Does Hein actually bring the culture of the spectacle into art institutions or does he merely highlight it? Are art institutions not already to some extent pervaded by this and indeed have been for some time? On the other hand, those of his works which seem to offer institutional critique also raise a number of other questions. Has this form of criticism itself not been part of a logic of economic exploitation for some time now? How can any kind of critical position be formulated from within a culture of spectacle?'.[1] Hein's work perpetuates and confronts this conundrum simultaneously, appealing equally to our critical and pleasurable faculties alike. *Maeve Polkinhorn*

Opposite page:
Spiral Labyrinth I 2006
High-polished mirror plate, aludibond, metal
Courtesy the artist and Johann König, Berlin

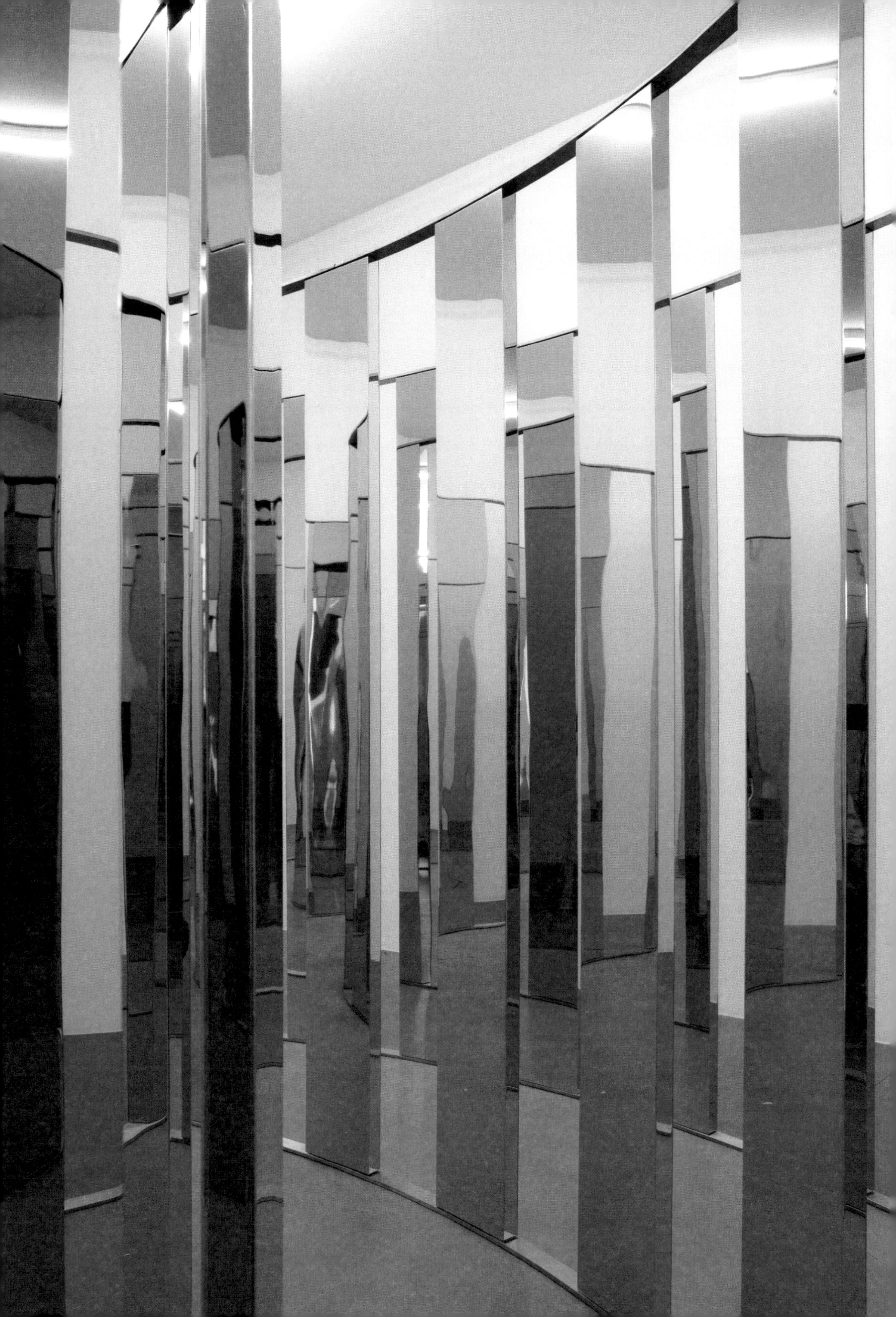

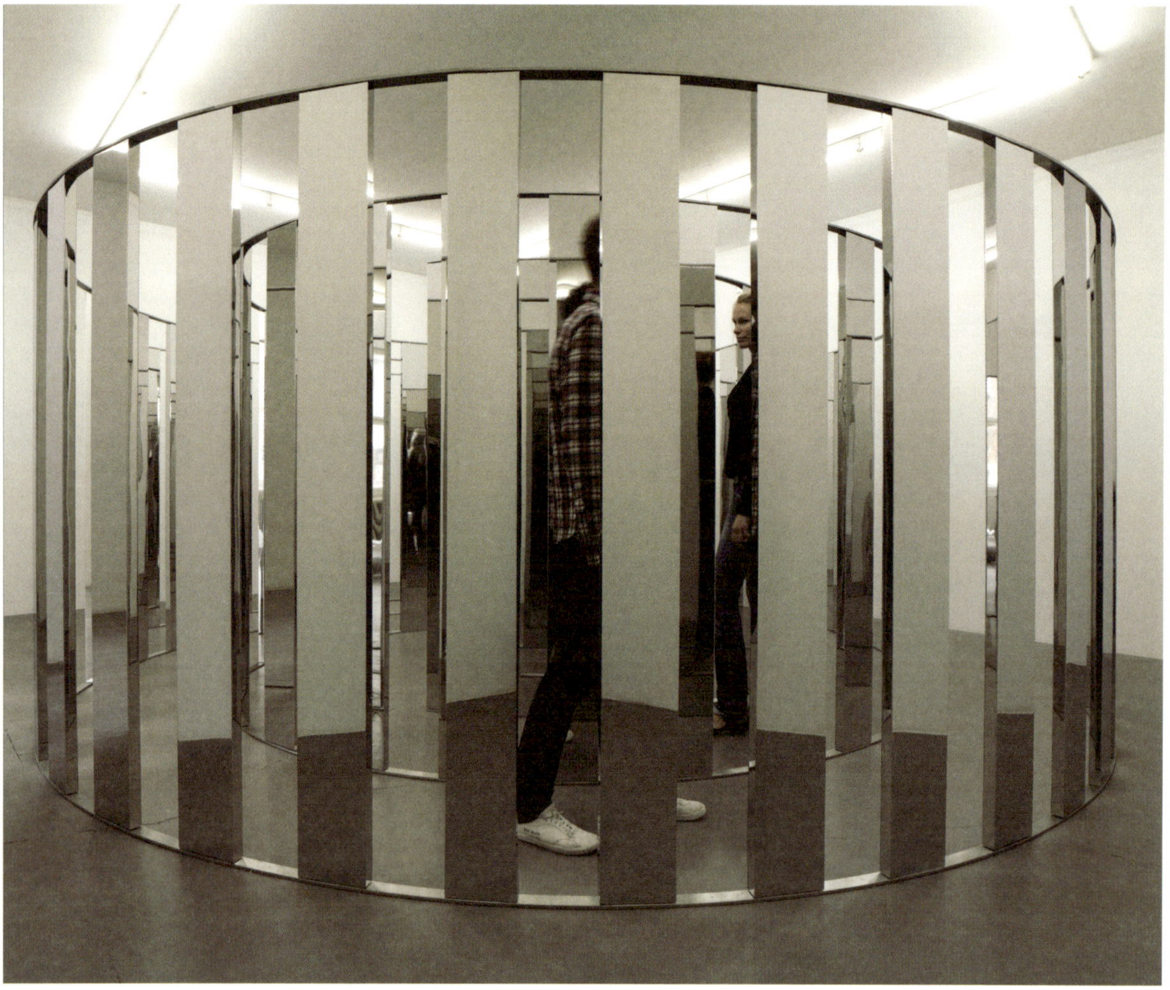

Spiral Labyrinth I 2006
High-polished mirror plate, aludibond, metal
Courtesy the artist and Johann König, Berlin

Hexagonal Water Pavilion 2007
Water, stainless steel, nozzles, electrical pumps, computer controller and wooden ramp
Fountain project for Enel Contemporanea, piazza Damiano Sauli, Rome 2007
Courtesy the artist and Johann König, Berlin

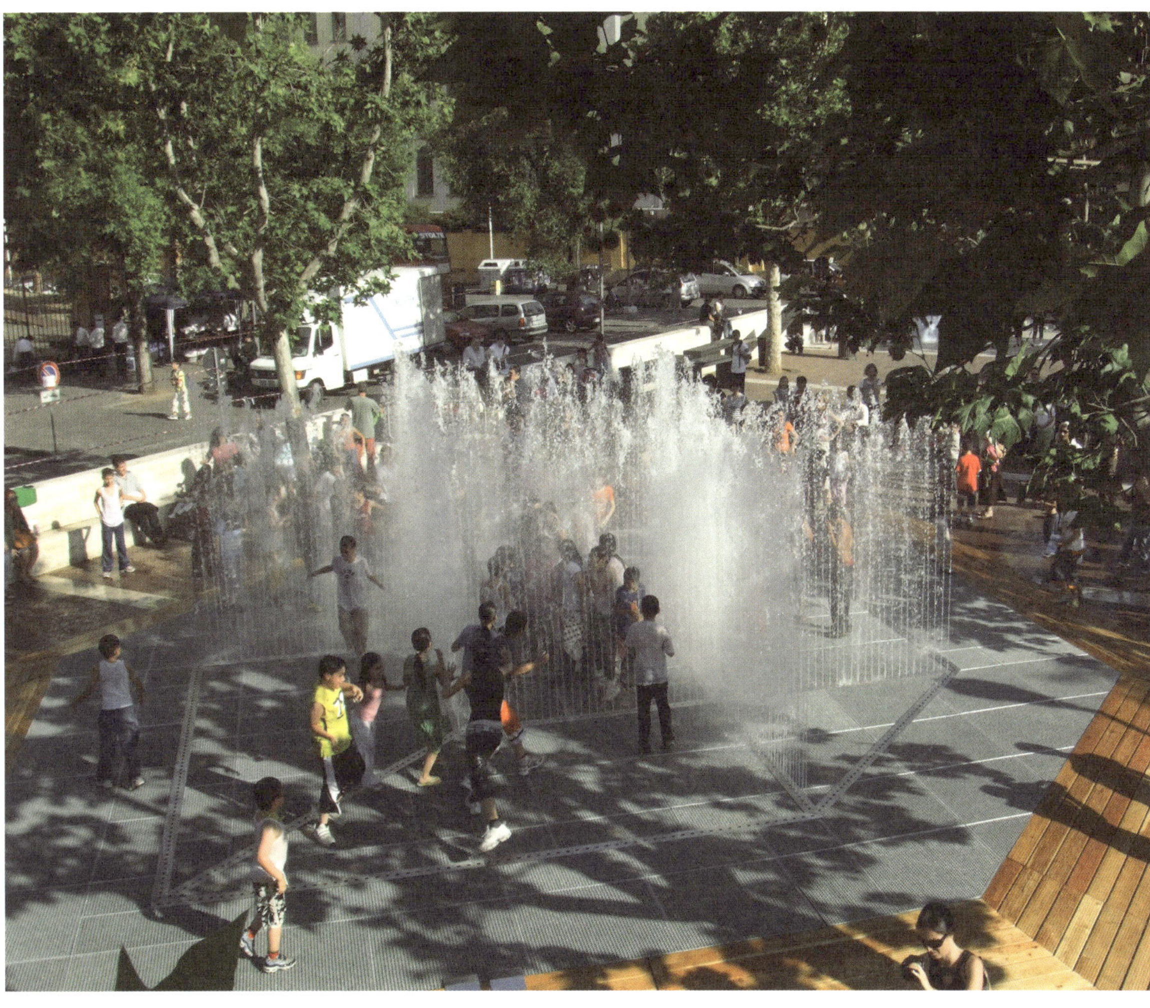

RENATA LUCAS

In Renata Lucas's practice, sites are the triggers for her imagination. She often departs from the formal qualities of inside or outside spaces to make interventions that slightly disturb their normal functioning, inviting gallery visitors, inhabitants of a neighbourhood or passers-by to experience those environments anew.

In *Barravento* 2001, Lucas built articulated wooden panels to cover the existing walls of the gallery. By hiding the architecture and adding a new flexible surface that multiplied the possibilities for different configurations, she broke down ideas of permanence and stability and brought to the fore oppositional ideas of ephemerality and transformation. Working with the same ideas in *Cruzamento* 2003, she brought the background, a large crossroads in front of a gallery in Rio de Janeiro, into the foreground as the protagonist of her work, through the simple action of covering it in plywood.

For *The World as a Stage*, Lucas intervenes in the site outside Tate Modern; in the garden that separates the building from the Thames walkway. A diagonally positioned section of a British wild forest will erupt within the garden, disrupting its existing vertical and horizontal rows of silver birch trees. Such sculptural interventions not only work as a formal comment on the site they inhabit, but are also evidence of a fictional narrative created through the artist's imaginary dialogue with the space. Not unlike Latin American novelists such as Jorge Luis Borges or Gabriel García Marquez, Lucas takes the site as a starting point for the invention of fiction, which will then be activated by the visitors. Common to her work are structures that express a desire to confuse the visitor's perception through multiple repetitions (*Mau Gênio* 2002) and infinite folds (*Falha* 2003) and therefore recall the idea of the labyrinth (*Comum de dois* 2002). In a recent commission for the 27th São Paulo Biennial, Lucas made *Quick Mathematics* 2006, an intervention in her own neighbourhood that consisted of adding a new pavement alongside the existing one, duplicating the lamp-posts, trees and flowerbeds so as to provoke a feeling of bewilderment or confusion in the minds of the Biennial visitors and the local residents.

In Lucas's installations, both the space of the gallery and the work itself are expanded beyond their traditional limits. Her work often negotiates with the social context in which the spaces in which she works are embedded. This social context can play as much of a role as the formal qualities of the architecture. In *Gentileza* 2005, an installation made for the artist-run space A Gentil Carioca, located in a house in a commercial area of Rio de Janeiro, Lucas took down the wall that separated the gallery from the recording studio next door, erasing the boundaries between the two spaces. In 2004, she made *Febre*, an installation that took place in a street a few blocks away from the Vermelho gallery. Here, Lucas parked a car that she covered with a modified trash basket, a commonly found object in the suburbs of São Paulo. She took away the car's radio and fixed it into the wall, making it available for passers-by to play music or news. Another car radio was also enigmatically fixed in a wall next to the gallery entrance. In this work, Lucas humorously played with the vernacular culture of the streets of São Paulo, staging a situation that actively involved both gallery visitors and city-dwellers.
Vanessa Desclaux

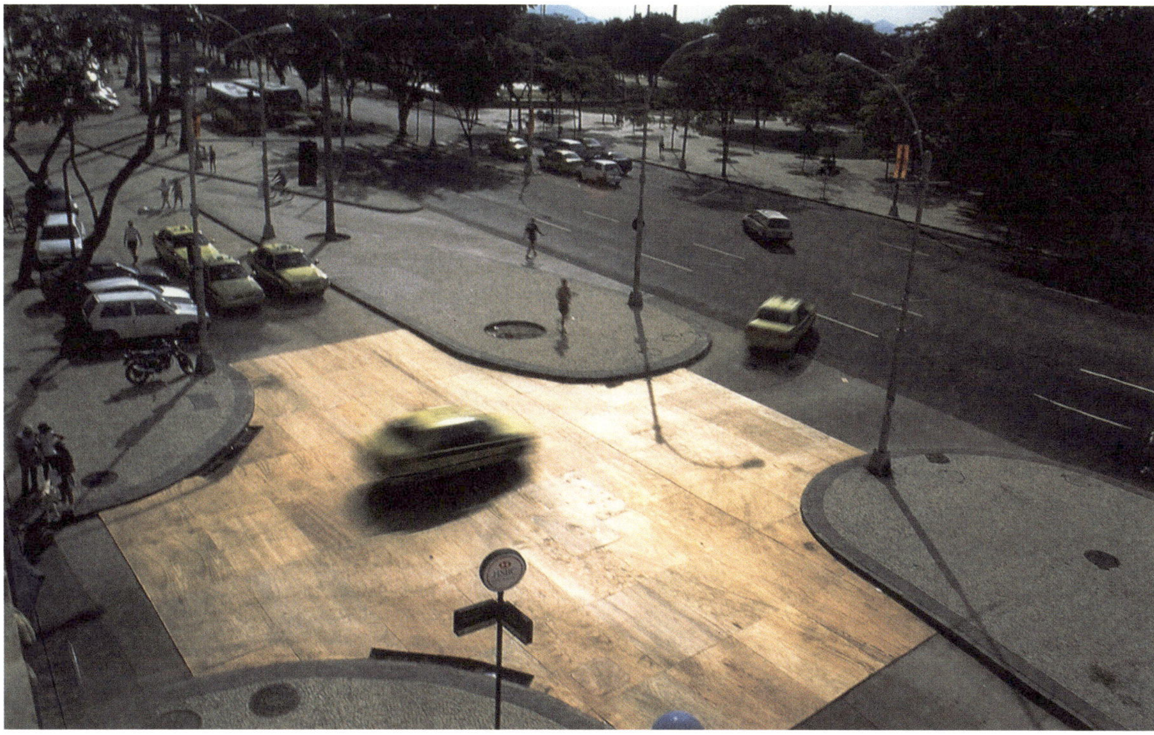

Cruzamento 2003
Plywood
Outside Centro Cultural Oduvaldo Viana Filho (Castelinho do Flamengo), Rio de Janeiro
Courtesy Galeria Luisa Strina, São Paulo

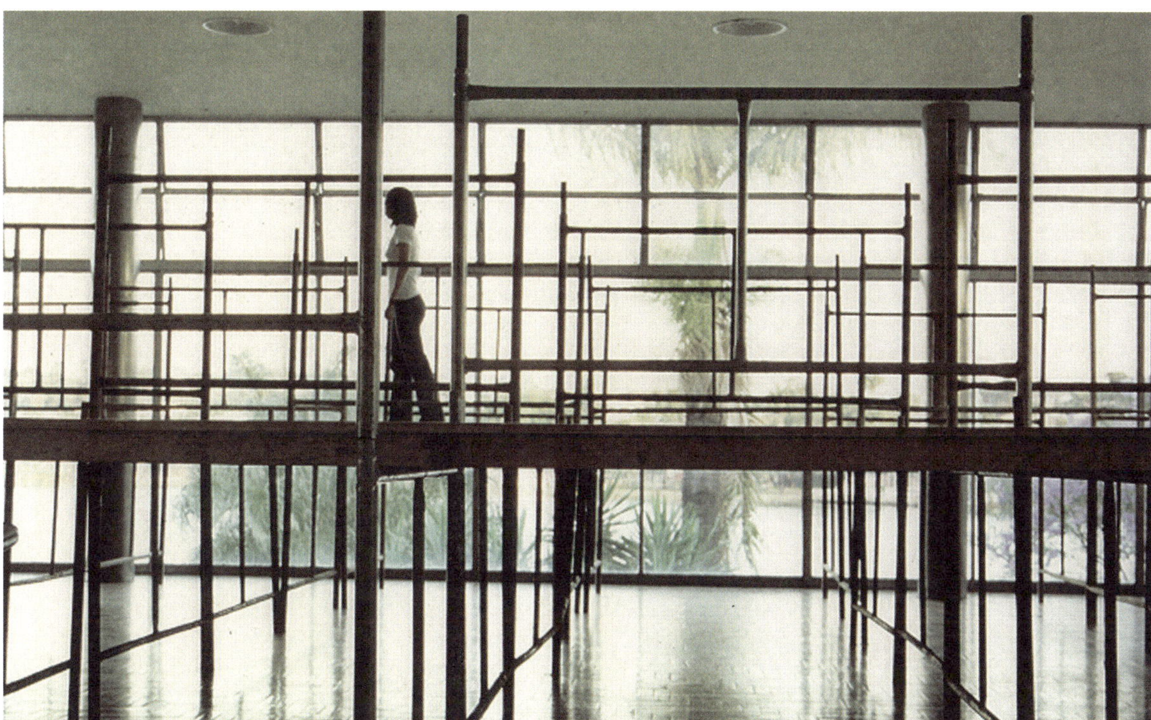

Mau Genio 2002
Scaffolding and plywood
Installation view at Museu de Arte da Pampulha, Belo Horizonte
Courtesy Galeria Luisa Strina, São Paulo

RITA MCBRIDE

Rita McBride creates illusions to emphasise the fabricated nature of reality. Best known for sculptural installations that reflect and critique the history of the visual environment, she has constructed replicas of classic modernist furniture and architectural details including space frames, pipes and skylights in materials traditionally associated with the fine arts or crafts. She has fabricated a full-sized Toyota chassis in rattan, and replicated Thonet bentwood chairs in Murano glass and shrink wrap. Reconsidering these everyday objects in unusual materials, McBride focuses the viewer's attention on their non-functional formal qualities.

Understanding the persuasive power of the media, McBride has also introduced fictional interventions including fake advertisements into the catalogues of her exhibitions. These play on enduring stereotypes and typologies, inviting a critical perspective on clichéd genres.

In 2000, McBride proposed a project for Vienna's Secession gallery, envisaging a skyscraper of luxury flats to be built on top of Olbrich's iconic building, pushing its gold dome towards the heavens. Re-appropriating architectural and design motifs from the past and applying them to a more cynical present, McBride's interventions question the utopian dreams of high modernism, the promise that clean lines and mod cons would advance a revolution of ideals and aesthetics.

McBride has referred to her sculptures as props, and the staged element of her work has been evident from early in her career. For an exhibition at the Michael Klein Gallery in New York in 1994, she created an installation based on the layout of the ground floor of Le Corbusier's Villa Savoye, incorporating her own sculptures into the interior in a way that recalled a stage set.

The following year, in collaboration with Benita-Immanuel Grosser, she made *The Studio Visit*. This work included a seating platform of three curved benches and a large spiral cardboard sail suspended from the ceiling with a series of cantilevered ropes. The work's appearance encouraged visitors to manoeuvre the ropes, but the sail remained perversely resistant to manipulation. The work's title alludes to a period before its construction and suggests that the pleasures and frustrations of collaborative participation extend to the interaction between artist and curator in realising an exhibition.

Extending some of the visual motifs and interactive potential of *The Studio Visit*, *Arena* is a large circular seating structure that mimics the layout and scale of an amphitheatre or sports stadium. Created as a series of identical modules designed to be reconfigured in different spaces as a temporary structure, the work is made of wood and Twaron, a material chosen for its lightness and strength. Despite its detailed construction and beautifully executed design, the work shifts the focus onto the empty stage in its centre, situating the viewer as protagonist. *Arena* was originally conceived for the Witte de With in Rotterdam in 1997, where it was installed in rooms surrounding the administration offices, drawing viewers' attention to the behind-the-scenes workings of the gallery. In this and subsequent displays, it also provided a site of potential interactions with other spectators. *Arena* encourages active, physical engagement and a shifting and peripheral viewpoint, in contrast with the traditionally more passive, focused perception of art in the museum space. *Rachel Taylor*

Opposite page:
Arena 1997
Twaron and wood
Installation, Sculpture Centre, Long Island City, New York, 2004
Courtesy of the artist and Alexander and Bonin, New York

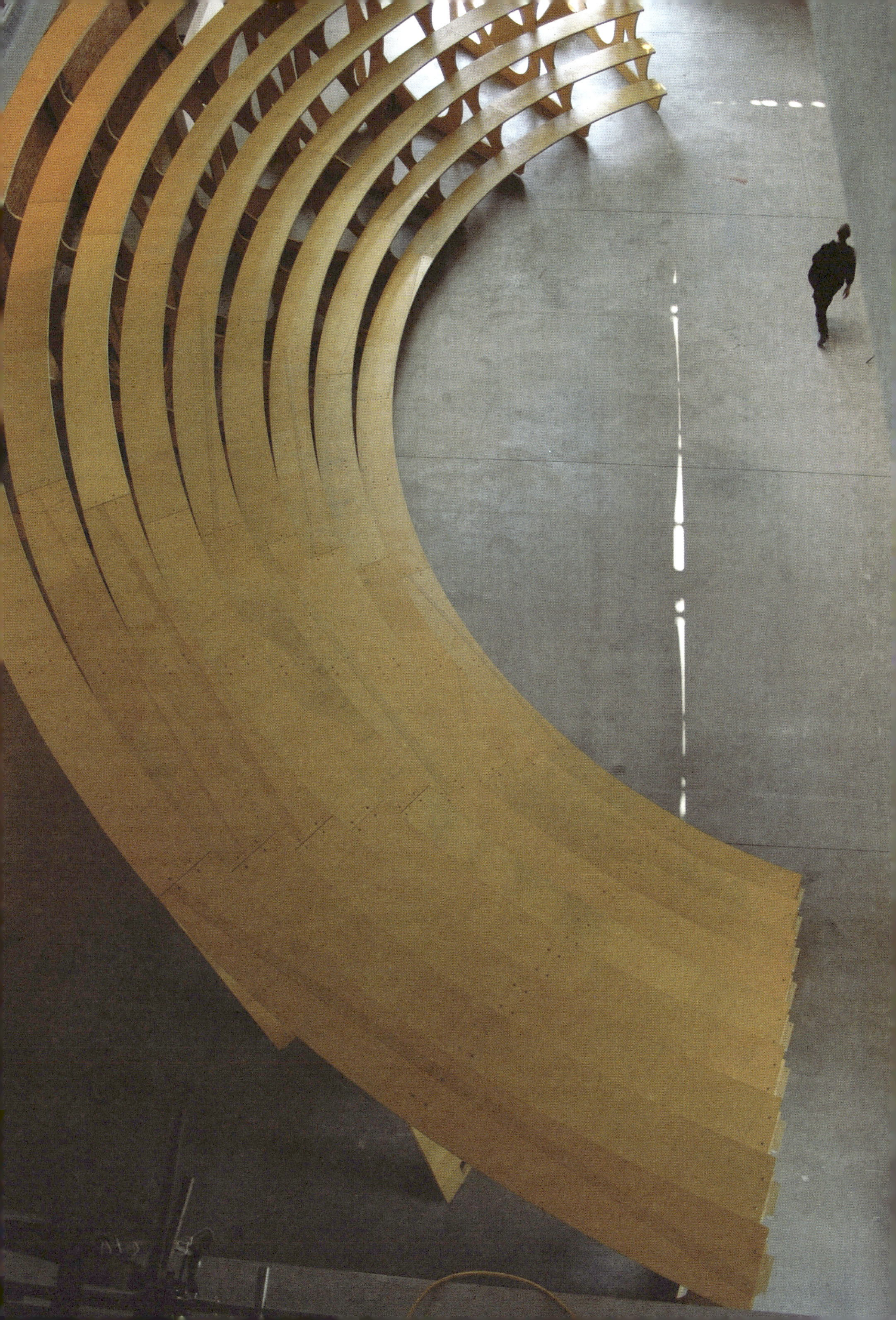

ROMAN ONDÁK

Roman Ondák brings about shifts or displacements in everyday situations. Sometimes the action he introduces is so subtle that it is almost invisible within the context in which it is 'performed'. *Resistance* 2006, for example, is a performance that took place at an exhibition opening. For this subtly subversive act that remained largely unnoticed, Ondák asked a number of people attending the event to leave their shoelaces untied. Similarly camouflaged within the everyday environment, *Good Feelings in Good Times* 2003 consisted of a queue of people that formed outside the main entrance of the Kunstverein in Cologne. The work was also performed at the Frieze Art Fair in October 2004, where the queue formed, dispersed and regrouped in various locations within the fair. The elusive nature of these performances means that they have a subsequent existence through rumour, imagination and memory.

These works, and others by the artist, initially exist as an idea manifested as a set of instructions, demonstrating Ondák's grounding in Conceptual art and the physical dematerialisation of the work. However, unlike many Conceptual works from the 1960s and 1970s that involve direct communication of an idea from the artist to the viewer, Ondák's works usually involve a third-party collaborator: the performer or producer. Through the collaborative nature of his work, Ondák provides a space for the performer / producer to contribute a personal interpretation of his instructions. The work thus becomes a dense network of interpretation and communication between artist, performer / producer and viewer. Occasionally, Ondák includes the curator in this network of dialogues. In *I'm just acting in it* 2007, for example, a number of people were asked to draw Ondák wandering through the empty gallery space, based solely on the curator's description of the artist.

Many of Ondák's works play with our perceptions of time and space. For *Silence, Please* 2004, at the Stedelijk Museum, Amsterdam, he asked the museum attendants to dress in guard uniforms from the period in which they were born, while *SK Parking* 2001 featured a cluster of old Slovakian Skoda cars, parked for two months behind Secession, a contemporary art museum in Vienna. These shifts or displacements serve to highlight notions of power and hierarchy not only within institutions but also in the wider social and political sphere. Whether through the expectant people queuing in *Good Feelings in Good Times*, or the many different fantasies of a future city represented in *Futuropolis* 2006, for which Ondák invited his friends and relatives to draw their vision of a megalopolis of the future, his works often embody acts of hope and desire. While sharpening our awareness of the here and now, Ondák's work also puts a poetic emphasis on the human capacity to envision new alternatives. *Maeve Polkinhorn*

Opposite page:
I'm just acting in it 2004
Series of ten drawings
Courtesy of the artist and Gallery Martin Janda, Vienna

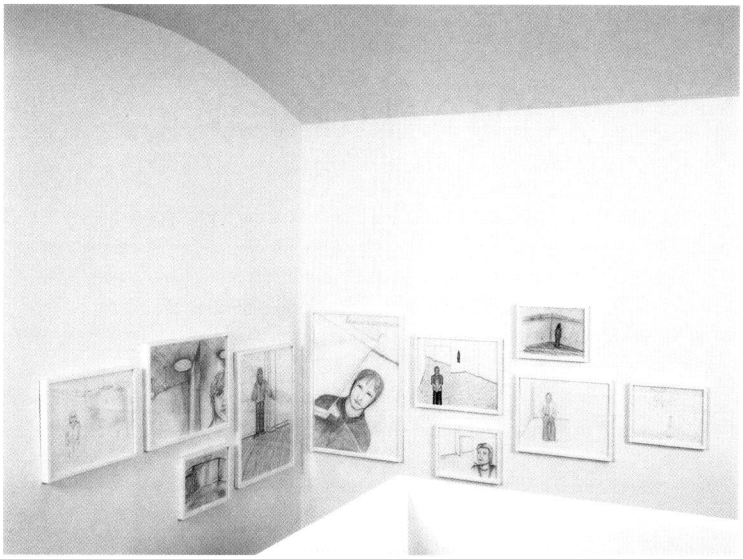

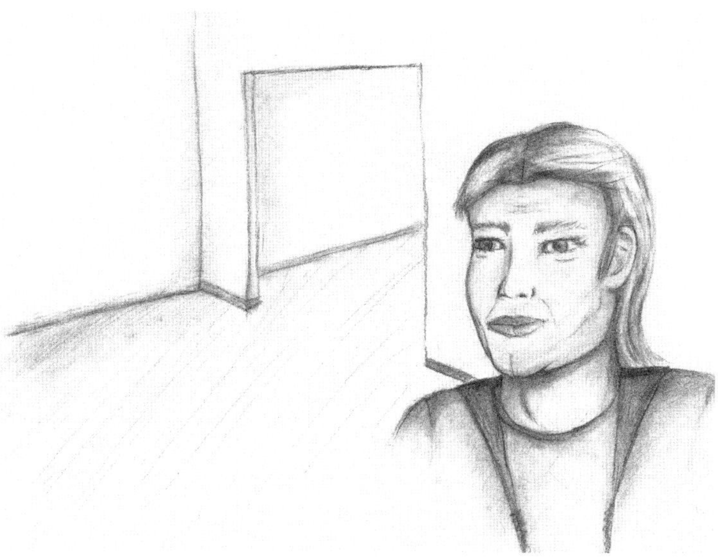

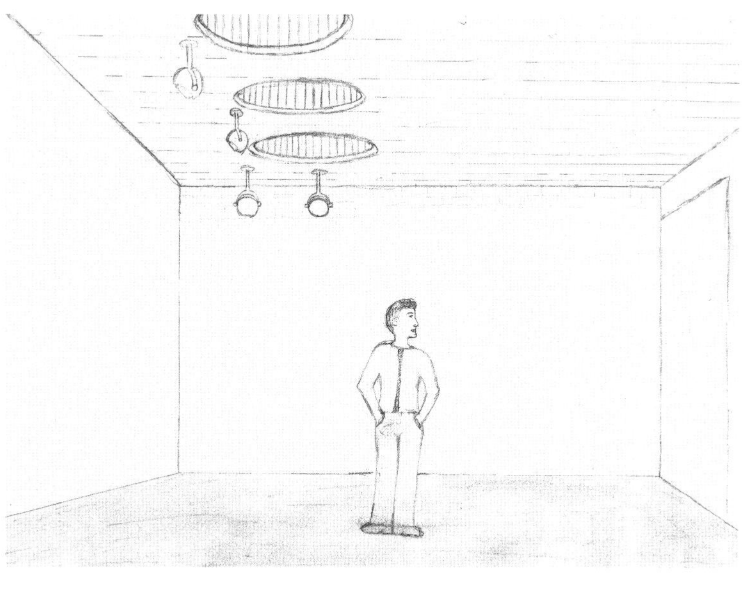

MARKUS SCHINWALD

The highly theatrical filmic, sculptural and image-based practice of Markus Schinwald takes the body as its starting point. He examines the body as object – how it moves, behaves and performs, and how its functionality is governed by items such as clothing or by abstractions like history or social mores. In most of his work, Schinwald's bodies are portrayed as objects without subjects, that is, as figures without emotions, personalities or characters, appearing instead to be possessed beings or automatons. Through them, Schinwald explores themes of Freudian psychoanalysis and, in particular, the relationship between the physical and the psychic.

The outdoor billboard work *Stage* 2000 foregrounds the notion of performance by featuring a red stage curtain pulled back to reveal two figures collaged into an otherwise barren interior. The seven vertical panels comprising the overall image are interchangeable and repeatable, allowing endless permutations of the staged scene to be installed around the city. In contrast, *Dictio pii* 2001 is a haunting, episodic film of seven people in a hotel. Emotionless and stoical, each person is subject to some sort of bodily manipulation by prosthesis, fetishistic contraption, or clothing modification. For example, one man applies a metal band to his head that forces the corners of his mouth into an eerie smile, while a woman has her hand suspended from a shoulder-mounted metal armature. These people move at an unhurried pace through vignettes of everyday activities like walking, dressing and smoking, occasionally interacting, but never communicating. Not only are their bodies subject to peculiar manipulations, but their whole persons seem to act out a perplexing choreography. Little is offered in the way of narrative or explanation, other than a proverb-like recitation by off-screen voices.

Costume alterations and bodily appliances without clearly defined functions also feature in a number of modified or 'falsely restored' Biedermeier-era etchings and paintings. Schinwald has exhibited the various fetishised contraptions themselves as curio objects for contemplation. *Contortionists* 2003 is a series of photographs of Taiwanese performers in various positions – aesthetic compositions portraying the limits of motion without mechanical assistance. Schinwald's more recent work has included life-size marionettes, which are in a way prosthetics of the whole body, disturbing substitutions for entire people.

One such puppet, *Otto* 2004, features in the film *Children's Crusade* 2004 as the automaton leader of a crowd of children through the streets of Vienna. The short movie-like fragment, with its storyline of the children gathering in mass behind the marionette, combines the semi-factual stories of a medieval children's crusade and *The Pied Piper of Hamlin*. In the first narrative, the children are manipulated into an ideological campaign, and in the second, are the unwitting victims of an act of revenge. With his equally ambiguous face, which rotates from eyes-open to eyes-closed, Otto is a disquieting leader, himself being manipulated by a hidden force. For *The World as a Stage*, Schinwald has fabricated a new marionette that is inhuman and unsettling, threatening the viewer with spurts of re-animation.

Cliff Lauson

Opposite page:
Stage 2000
Installation views
Courtesy of the artist and Georg Kargl, Vienna

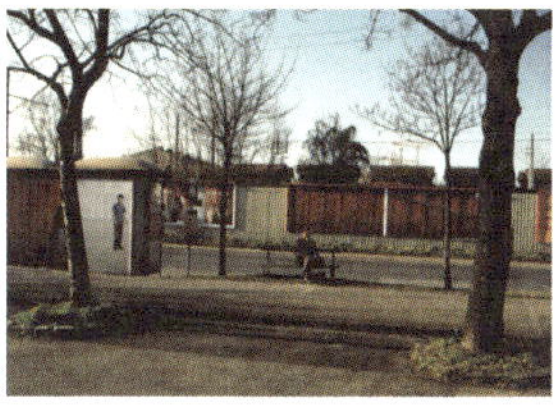
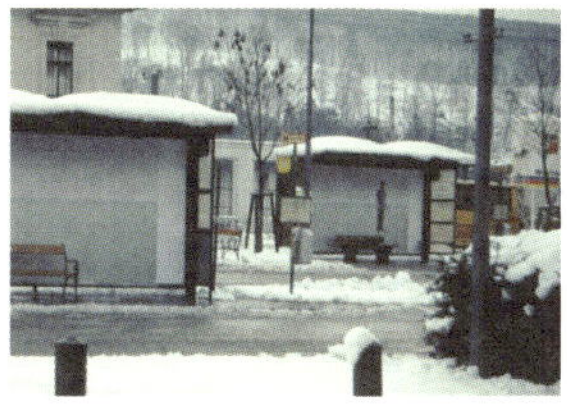
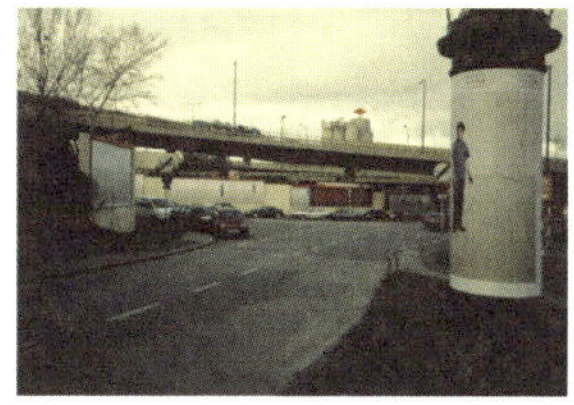
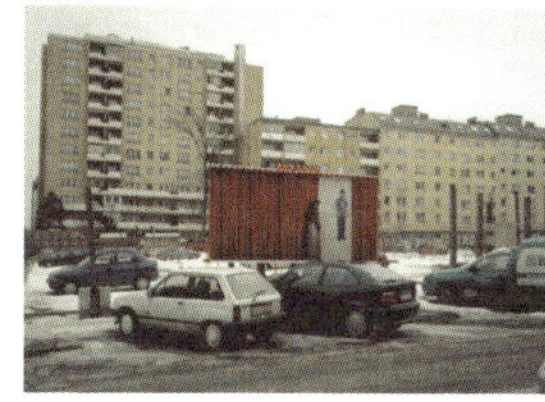
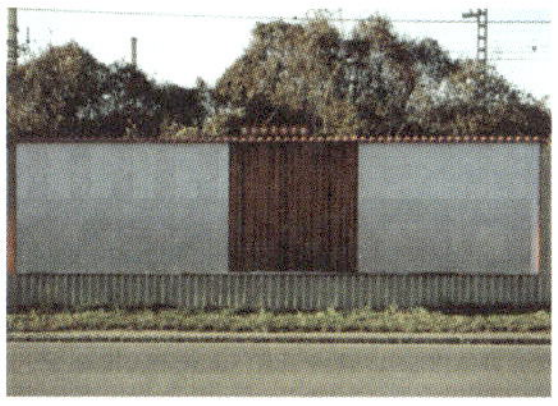
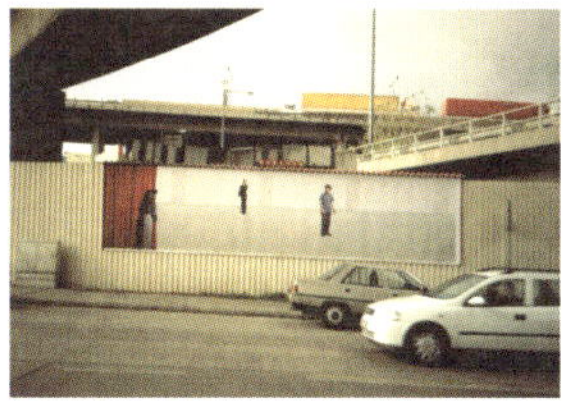
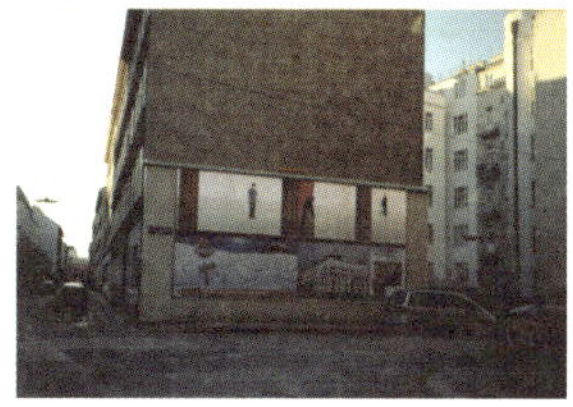
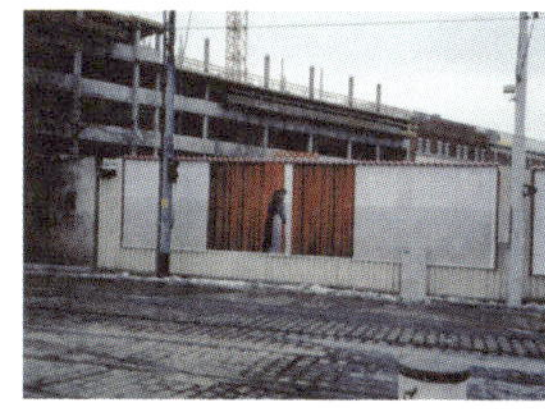
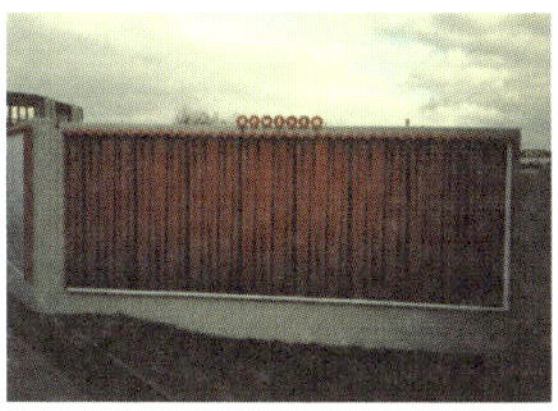
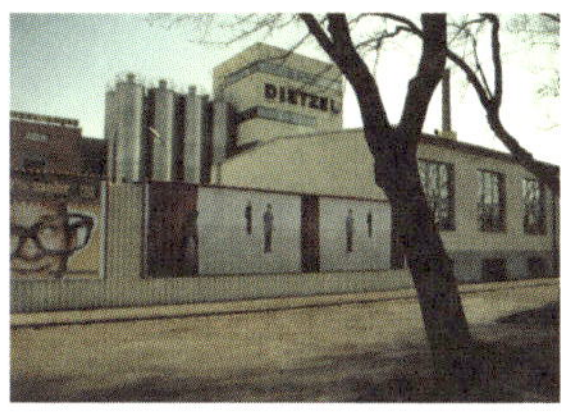
DIETZEL
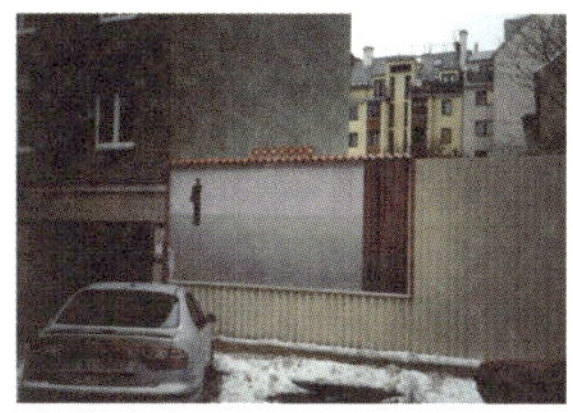
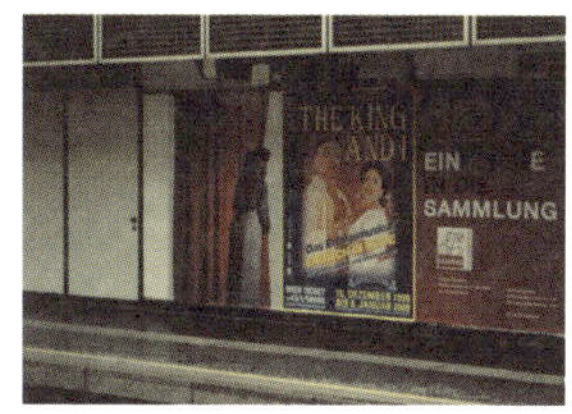
THE KING AND I
EIN E
SAMMLUNG
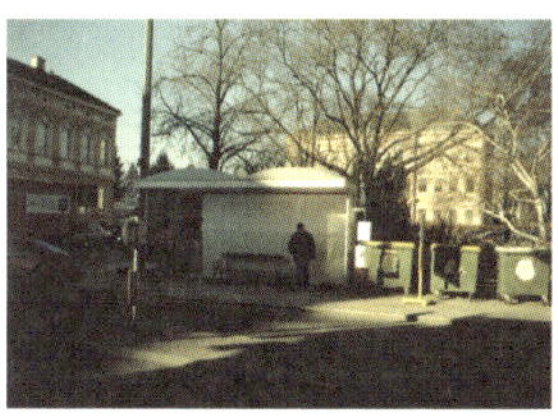
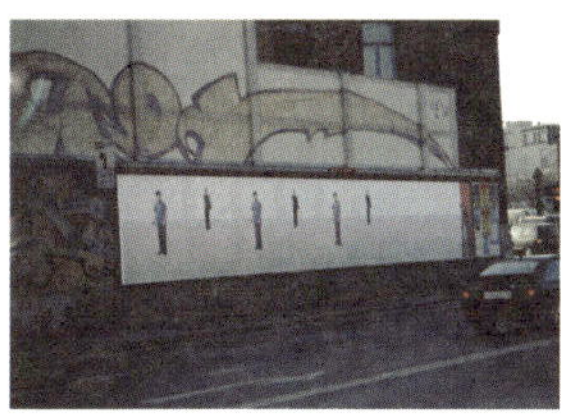
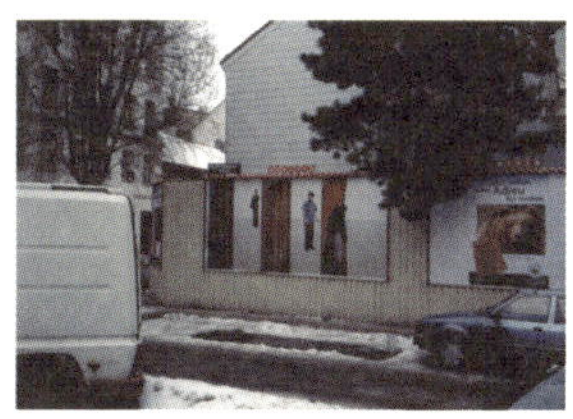
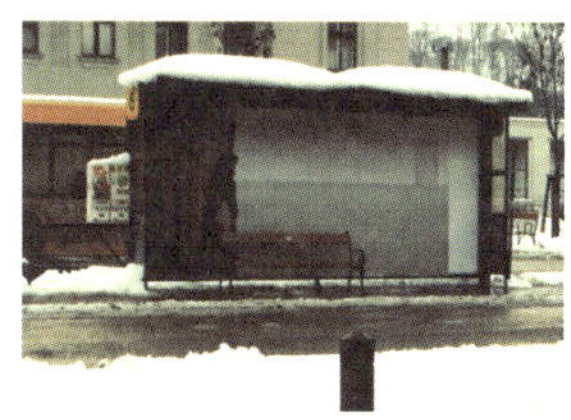
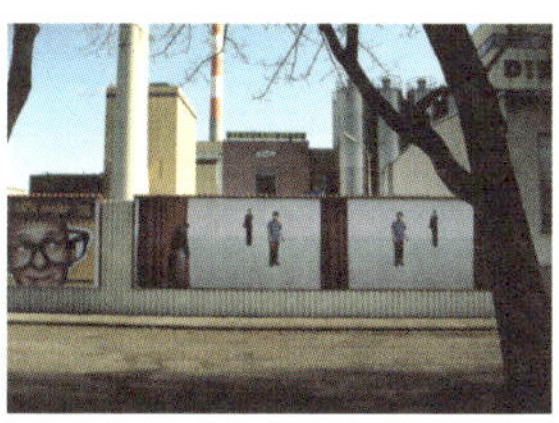
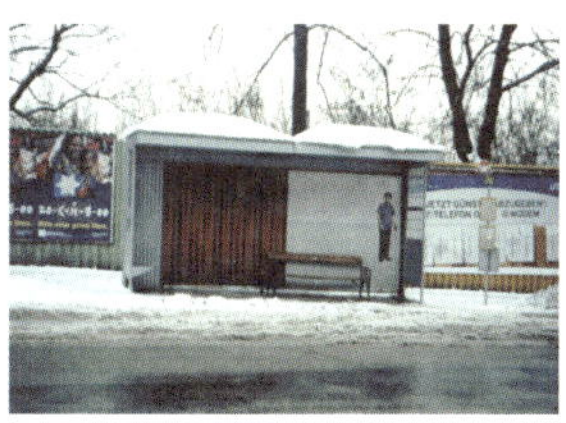
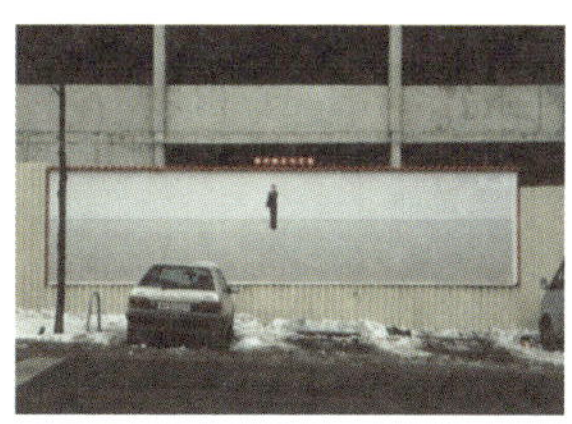
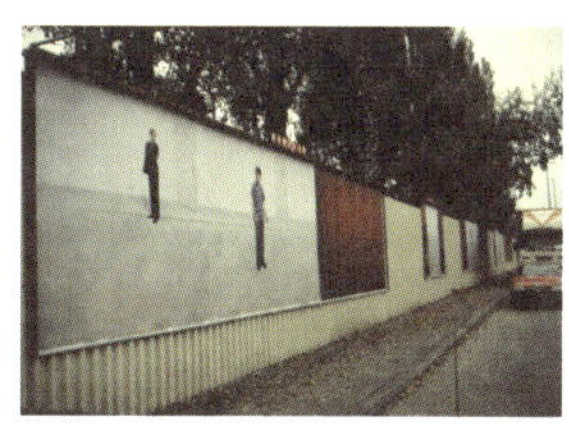
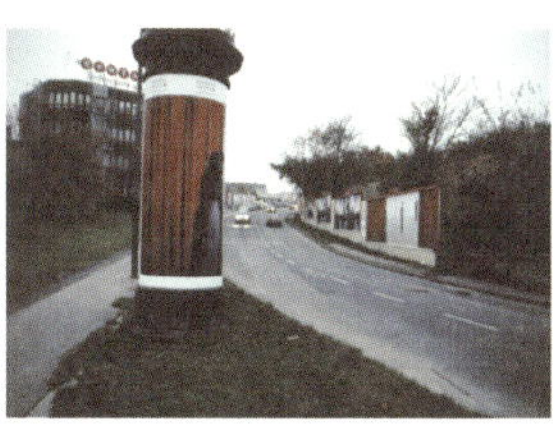
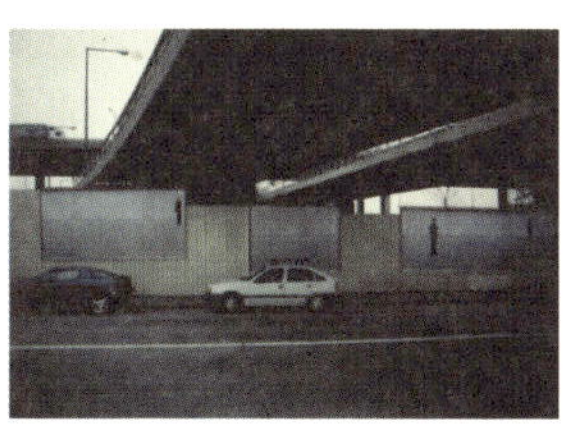
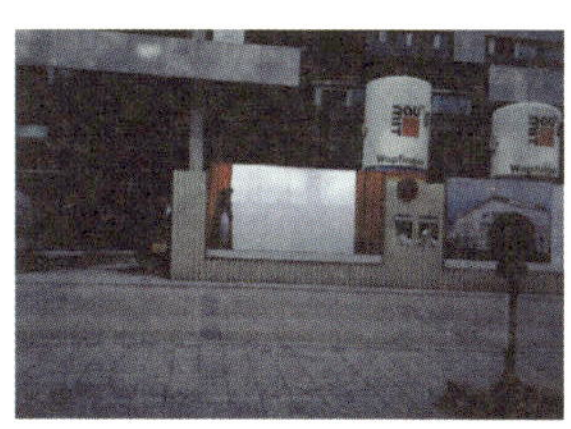
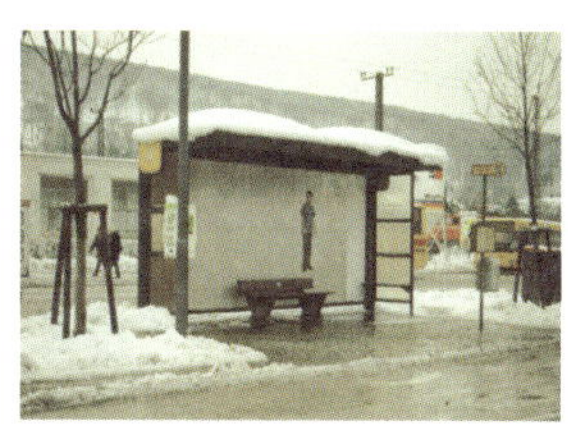
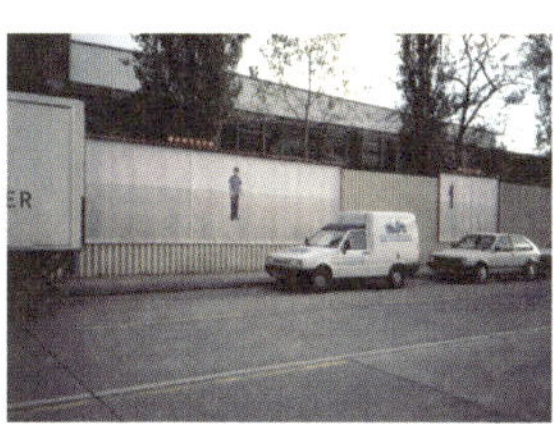
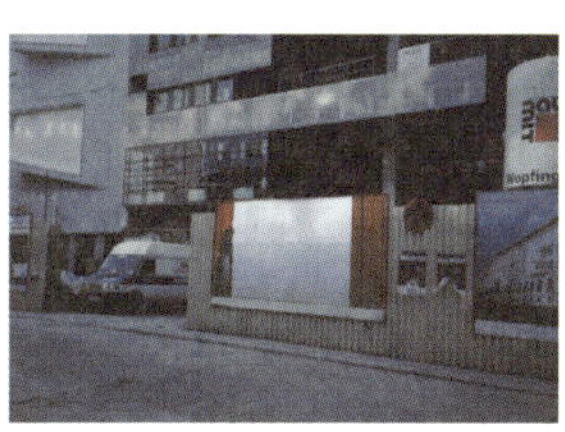
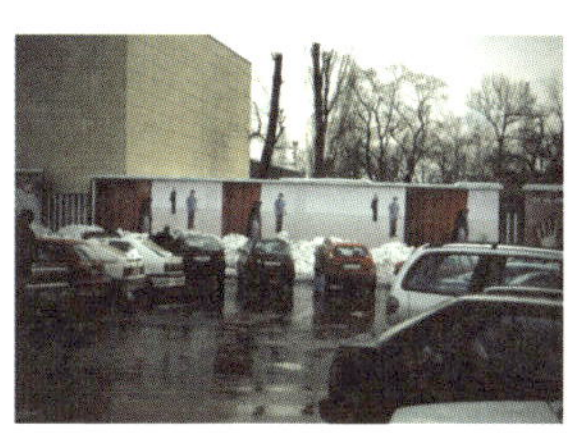
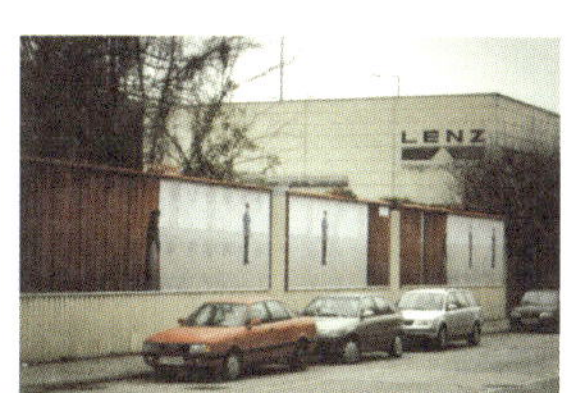
LENZ
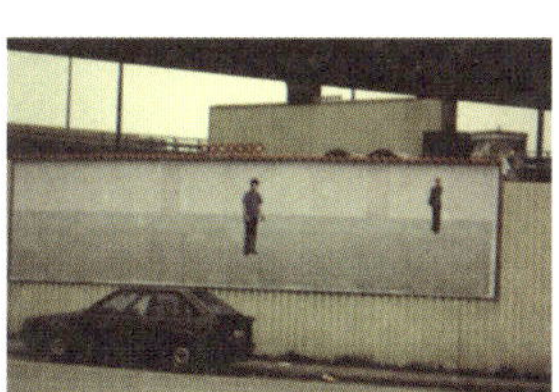
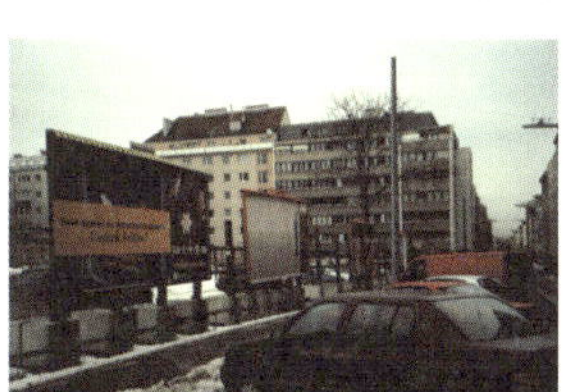
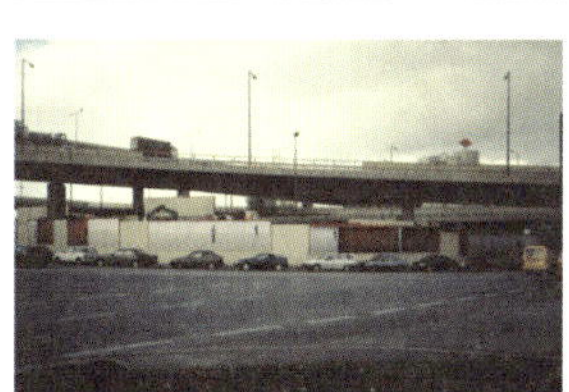
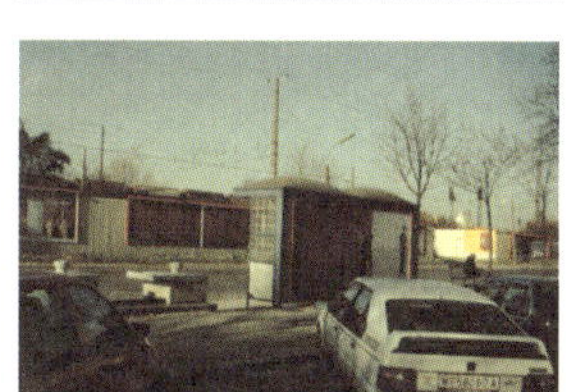

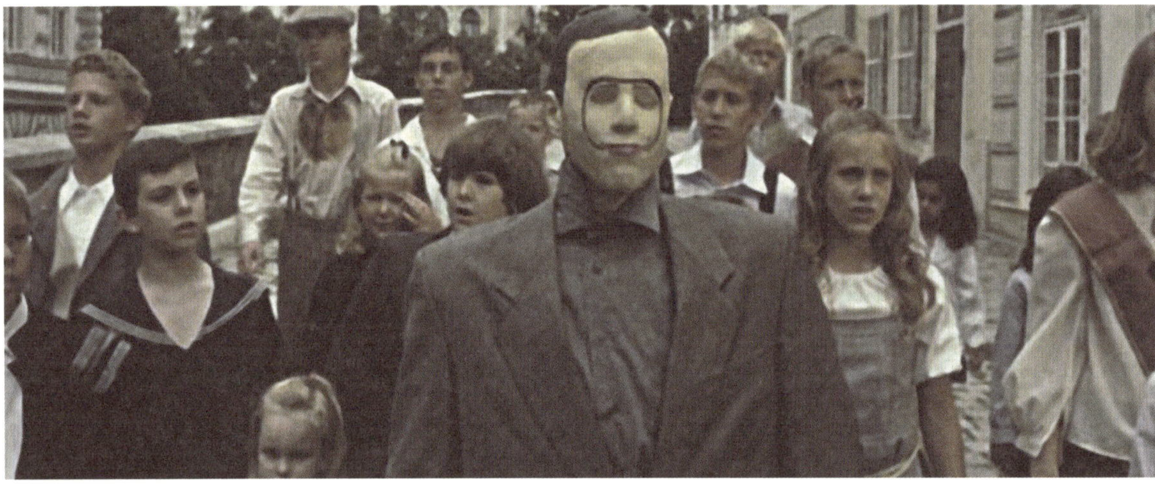

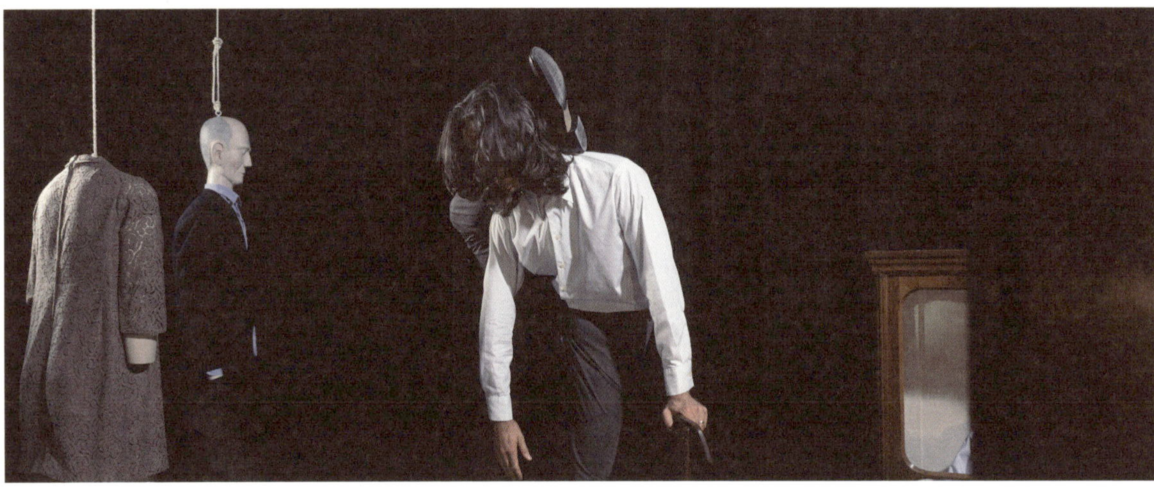

MARKUS SCHINWALD
Top:
Children's Crusade 2004
Video
Courtesy of the artist and Georg Kargl, Vienna

Bottam:
Contortionists (tait) 2006
C-print
Courtesy of the artist and Georg Kargl, Vienna

TINO SEHGAL

In Tino Sehgal's *This is new* 2003, on display in *The World as a Stage*, a gallery assistant sits at the entrance of the exhibition to check visitors' tickets and hand them a leaflet. During that brief exchange, the gallery assistant looks at the visitor and speaks out loud a headline from a daily newspaper of his or her choice. If the visitor responds to the intervention, the invigilator repeats the headline and states: '*This is new*, Tino Sehgal, 2003.' If the visitor does not react, this is the end of the exchange and the nature of the intervention, i.e. that it is a work of art, is not clearly revealed. *This is new* is an example of how Sehgal consciously plays with theatricality by building a frame and creating a context within which unexpected encounters could take place. Tim Etchells of Forced Entertainment refers to theatre as 'a frame (game) constructed so that people can look at other people… [offering] deceptively transparent unfolding vantage points on the faces, bodies and movements of human beings.'[1] Unlike theatre, Sehgal's choreographed situations are not meant for people to 'look' at other people but invent a space where people physically and emotionally relate to other people differently.

Sehgal has developed a body of works that investigate the two-fold process of a simultaneous 'production' and 'deproduction' through the transformation of actions. In this sense, he applies the process that defines dance as a discipline to the field of visual art. He has also directed his practice towards a critique of the production of material objects through the transformation of materials. His 'situations' challenge the visual arts by refusing the production of any object, documentation or written trace (no video or photography, no written instructions, not even a written act of sale). If Conceptual art through its attempt to dematerialise the art object succeeded in shifting the focus from object to process, Sehgal sets up a new series of parameters and addresses the question of economic production, showing that his concern does not lie in the issue of the commodified and fetish quality of art works. His work rather intends to propose alternative and more sustainable ways of production.

Sehgal's pieces follow the temporality of the exhibition and exist immaterially from the moment of their creation. Within this conceptual framework, his situations rely on the bodies of the 'interpreters' as raw material. In his various works, these have been, dancers,[2] singers,[3] museum guards,[4] children,[5] or people working in cultural production.[6] The interpreters transform Sehgal's oral instructions into ephemeral but infinitely repeated actions that create a space where the viewer could engage in an intellectual and physical encounter. In *This Progress* 2006,[7] each visitor was invited by interpreters to take part in individual discussions on the subject of 'progress' and taken on a dramatic journey through the galleries, halls, back corridors and stairs of the Institute of Contemporary Arts in London. In *This is new*, this encounter is much more subtle and, in that sense, perhaps more perplexing. It might leave the visitor with a confused idea of what just happened. The visitor might try to restage the uncertain experience by coming back into the exhibition, yet will implicitly know that each encounter will be different. *Vanessa Desclaux*

CATHERINE SULLIVAN

Catherine Sullivan takes theatre as her conceptual paradigm, exploring it as a visual form both from an aesthetic and an anthropological perspective. Working across film, installation and performance, she investigates the act of performing itself. Her work crosses the boundaries between theatre, cinema, dance and the visual arts to explore individual empowerment, social trauma and economic and political situations.

Sullivan's performances, for films or on stage, might be characterised as excessive and baroque. She makes exhaustive use of the materials she uses, such as gestures, attitudes and emotions, as well as music, decor and costumes, 'until [her] political or poetic concerns are met or [she starts] to generate interesting effects'.[1] However, her transformation of these elements can also be described as a very formal enterprise directed towards visual abstraction. In *Big Hunt* 2002, for example, she restaged five scenes taken from films, applying to each scenario five different 'economies', or styles of acting. In *The Chittendens: The Resuscitation of Uplifting* 2005, the actors' performances are regimented by a complex score combining movements and attitudes to be performed according to different parameters of time, dramatic effects and physical form. This choreographic method, which she terms 'D-Pattern', was inspired by Minimalist music compositions from the 1960s, and developed in collaboration with the composer Sean Griffin. It evolved in response to Sullivan's desire to create a system that would analytically determine the combination of different narrative elements such as history, character, action or style in her work.

Sullivan's analytic approach, informed by an anthropological and historical knowledge of theatre and performance, creates a structure within which she weaves a complex constellation of cultural and historical references, translated into visual form through the filter of the artist's imagination. Griffin describes this dense collage of ideas, references and images as follows: 'For the Chittendens Suite, the core concept was already a shaky amalgam: *Nautical-Modernica*. Nautical meaning tonal, heavily coded in history, colonialism, over-wrought emotionality, and nineteenth century desire; *Modernica* meaning a kind of pre-fabricated, atonal, angular, rational but abstract style.'[2]

Sullivan has developed a unique perspective on the human condition through the lens of performance and its artificial masks. By focusing so intensely on acting techniques, isolating gestures, emotions and attitudes from their original contexts and introducing them again within highly composed choreographies, she strips away the real to reveal the artifice. Deliberately inverting the experience, training and skills of the actors who perform in her films and theatre pieces, Sullivan pushes the notion of acting to an extreme where, in a process of disembodiment, only the character's 'style' or mask is visible, preventing the spectators from entering into any kind of emotional identification with them. *Vanessa Desclaux*

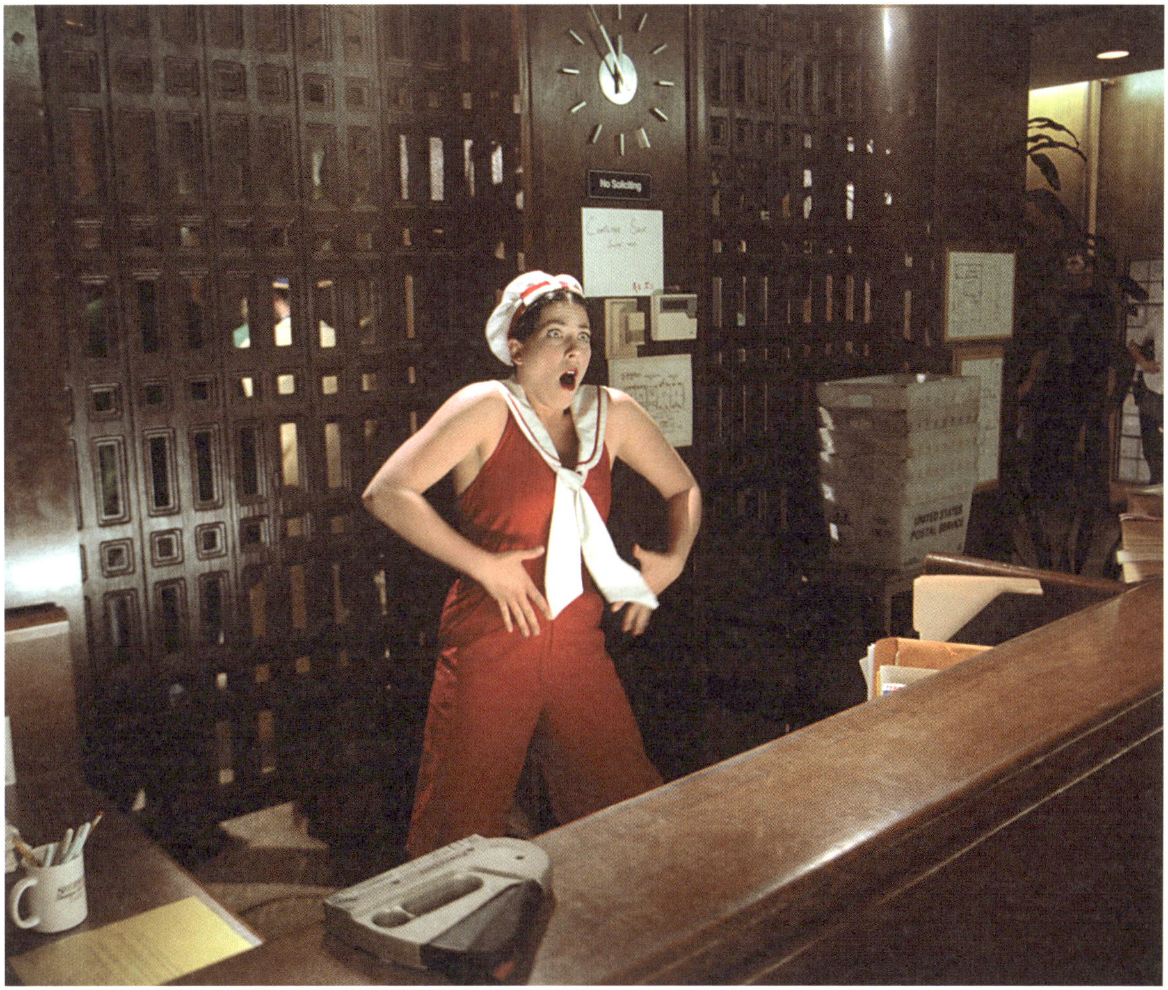

The Chittendens: The Resuscitation of Uplifting 2005
DVD
Tate, purchased with funds provided by the 2006 Outset Frieze Acquisitions Fund for Tate 2007
Courtesy of the artist and Galerie Catherine Bastide, Brussels

Following page:
Ice Floes of Franz Joseph Land (Orensanz Manifestation) 2004
Performance
Angel Orensanz Center, New York
Courtesy of the artist and Galerie Catherine Bastide, Brussels

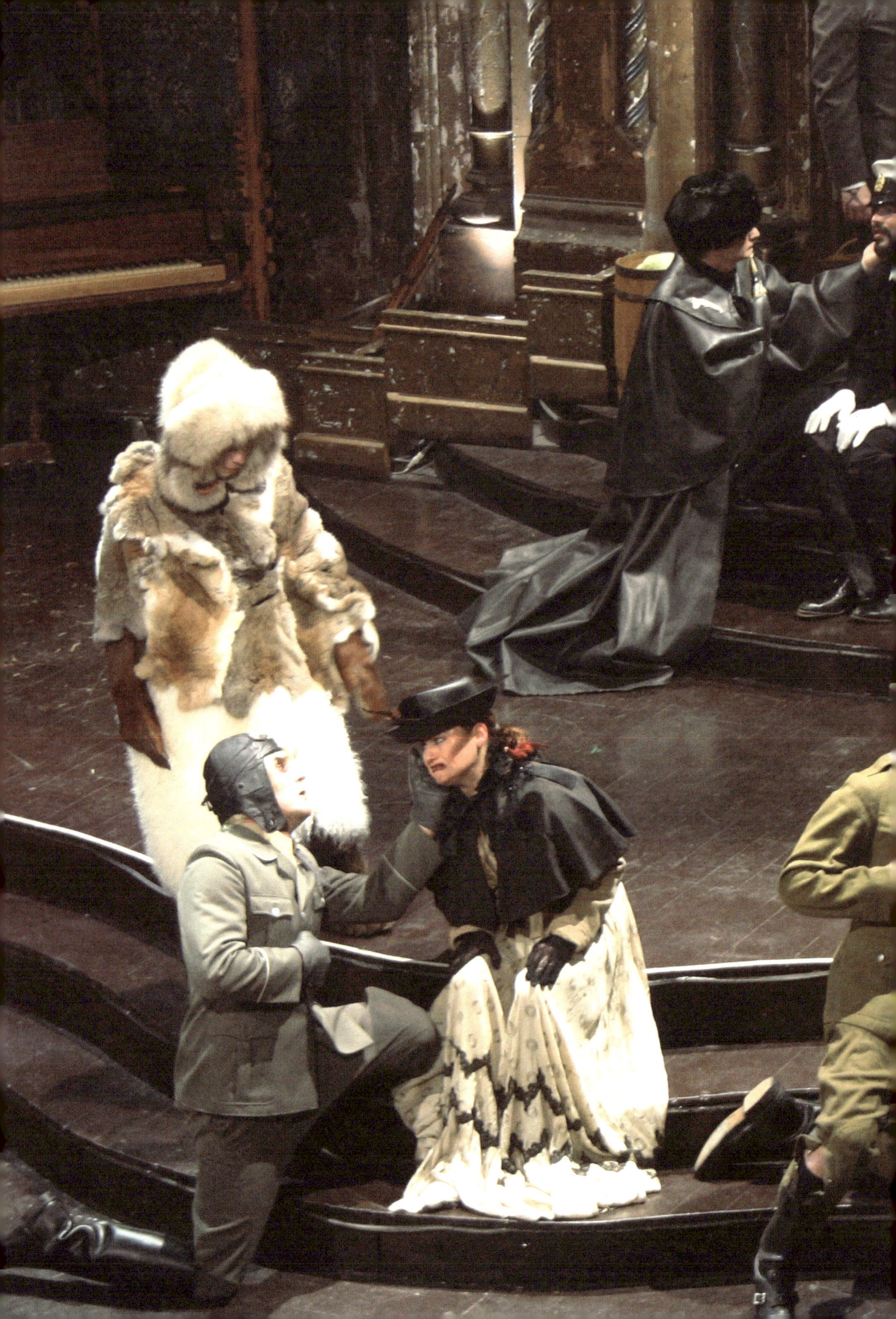

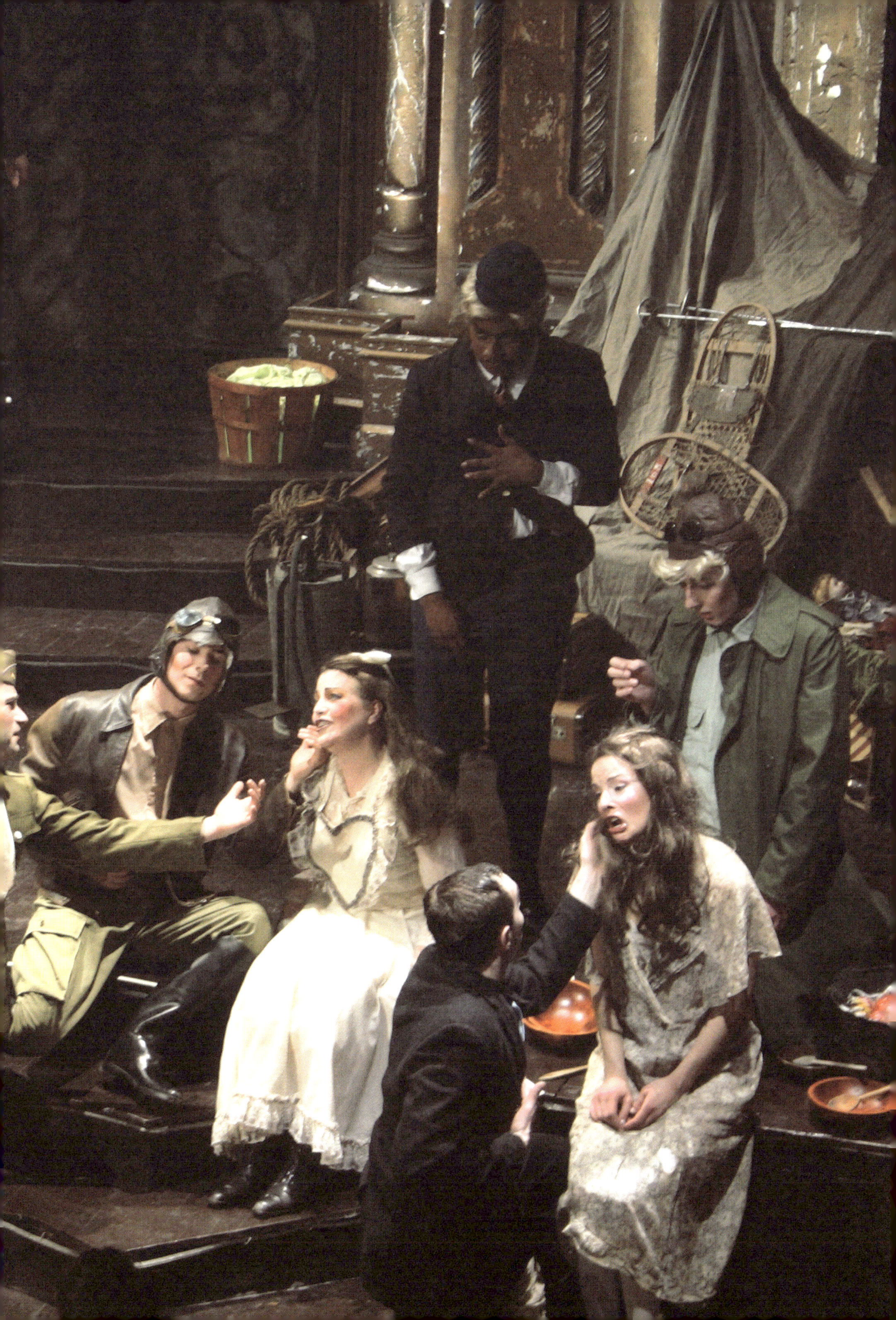

MARIO YBARRA JR.

Mario Ybarra Jr. works across a range of media, drawing inspiration from popular culture, particularly the rich intermingling of North and Latin American culture in his native southern California. *Brown and Proud* 2006, a large-scale mural commissioned for the exhibition *Alien Nation* at the Institute of Contemporary Arts, London, features two iconoclastic figures: the Mexican revolutionary Emiliano Zapata and Chewbacca from the *Star Wars* films. Appropriating and conflating Latino and American culture, history and fiction, politics and entertainment, the mural is a witty comment on the diverse influences on contemporary Chicano identity.

Go Tell It is a series of staged photographs depicting the artist with a megaphone, pumping his fist in the air. The images appear to document acts of protest, but their message is deliberately oblique. Ybarra uses the poses of political action as a personal vocabulary, leaving it up to the viewer to decode the message he imparts.

Equally at home on the streets and in the museum, Ybarra's socially engaged practice includes leading art workshops in his local community, curating shows by other artists and frequent collaborations. In an installation in the Los Angeles County Museum of Art in 2006, he commemorated the destruction of the Belmont Tunnel. The trolleys that used this subway tunnel were decommissioned in 1955. In the years after its abandonment the tunnel provided a makeshift shelter for the homeless and from 1983 provided a rich site for graffiti art. Ybarra's installation included a cave-like structure recalling the tunnel's entrance decorated by graffiti artists Rick One and Prime. The installation also included a video documenting the history of Belmont Park and a Mayan sculpture from LACMA's collection showing figures playing a ball game similar to tarasca, which is still practiced in the park today.

The performative element of Ybarra's work has taken the form of discrete actions and relational interventions. In one of his first mature works, Ybarra borrowed a friend's 1979 Chevrolet Monte Carlo, which had been customised in homage to the Dallas Cowboys, and drove the car down Broadway in downtown Los Angeles. *Cowboys on Broadway* 2002 focused attention on the absence of a main street and a local football team in America's second-largest city. For *The Peacock Doesn't See Its Own Ass/ Let's Twitch Again: Operation Bird Watching in London* 2006, Ybarra and his wife Karla B. Diaz used the Serpentine Gallery in Kensington Gardens, London, as the base for a bird-watching club. He encouraged participants to focus on non-native birds in the park, making a subtle comment on immigration.

In 2002, Ybarra co-founded the art collective Slanguage, which provides engaged art outreach programmes for young people in the working-class neighbourhood of Wilmington. A recent offshoot of this project was an exhibition of art by prisoners staged in The New China Town Barbershop, a gallery set up by Ybarra and Diaz in a former barbershop in LA's Chinatown. A full-scale reproduction of the barbershop, featuring Ybarra's drawings, forms the centrepiece of his contribution to *The World as a Stage*. In a nod to the exhibition's London setting, the artist has titled the installation *Sweeney Tate*, recalling the infamous fictional demon barber of Fleet Street. The installation will provide a setting for London barbers to ply their trade during the course of the exhibition.
Rachel Taylor

Opposite page:
The New Chinatown Barbershop 2006
Installation view, Los Angeles County Fair
Courtesy of the artist and Anna Helwing Gallery, Los Angeles

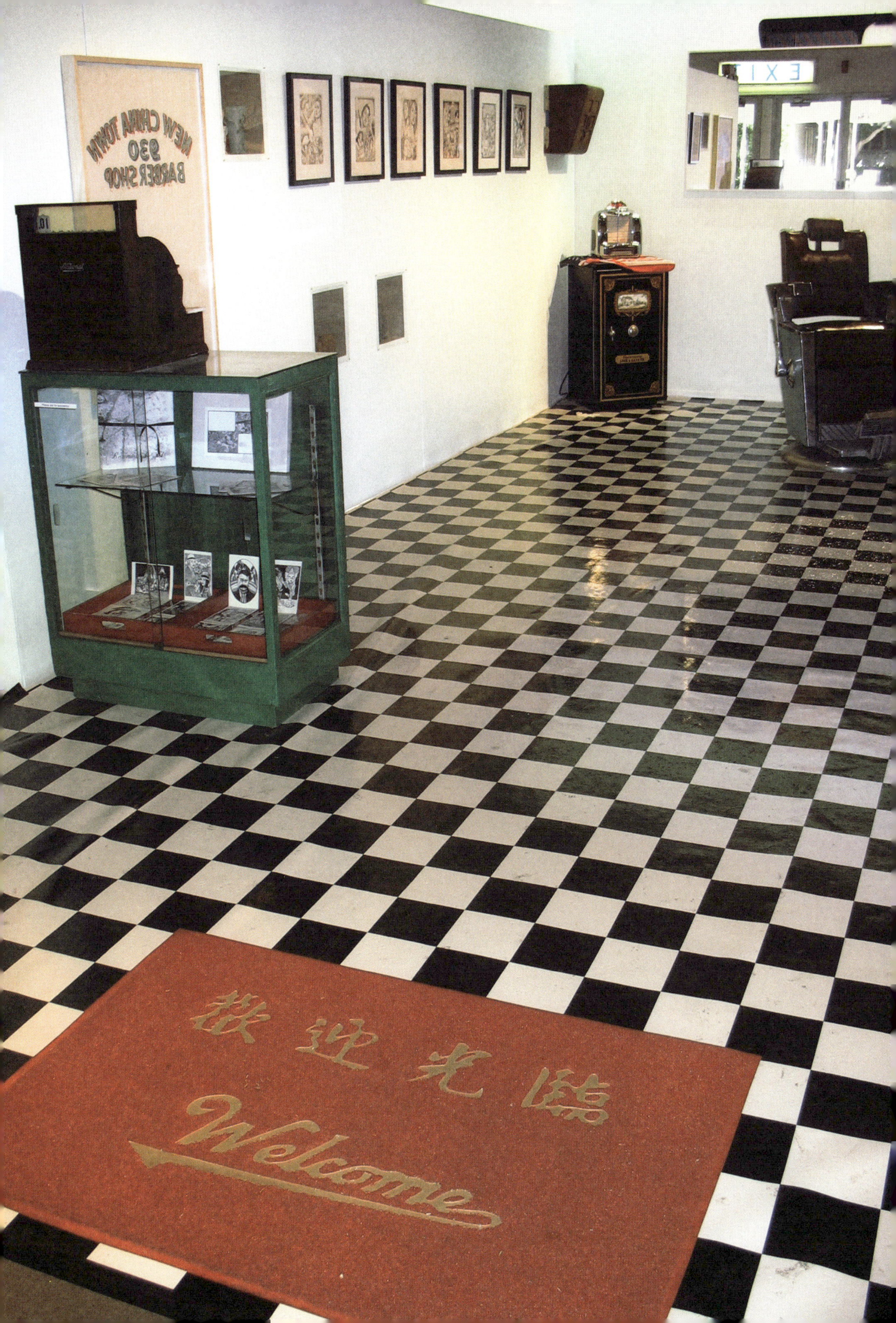
NEW CHINA TOWN
930
BARBER SHOP
EXIT
歡迎光臨
Welcome

Belmont Ruins 2006
Installation view, LACMA Lab
Courtesy of the artist and Anna Helwing Gallery, Los Angeles

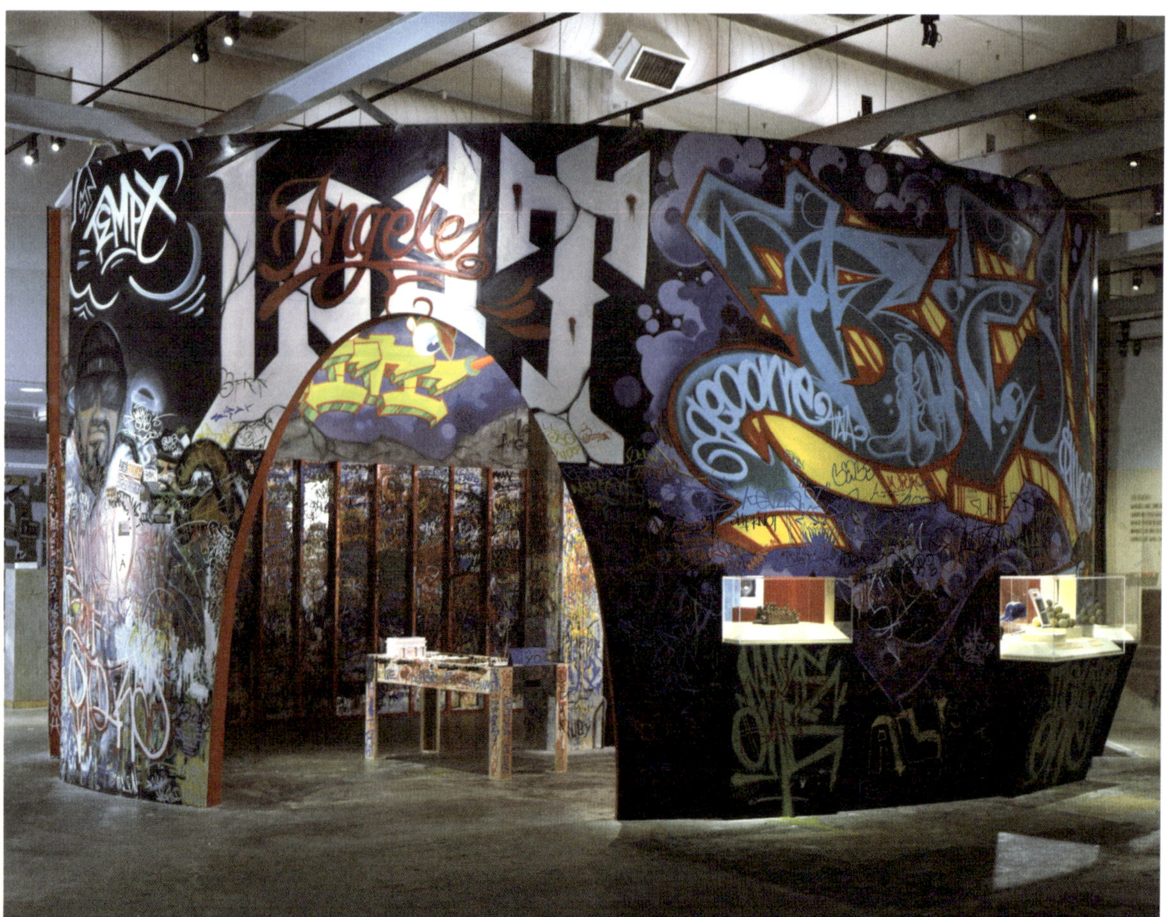

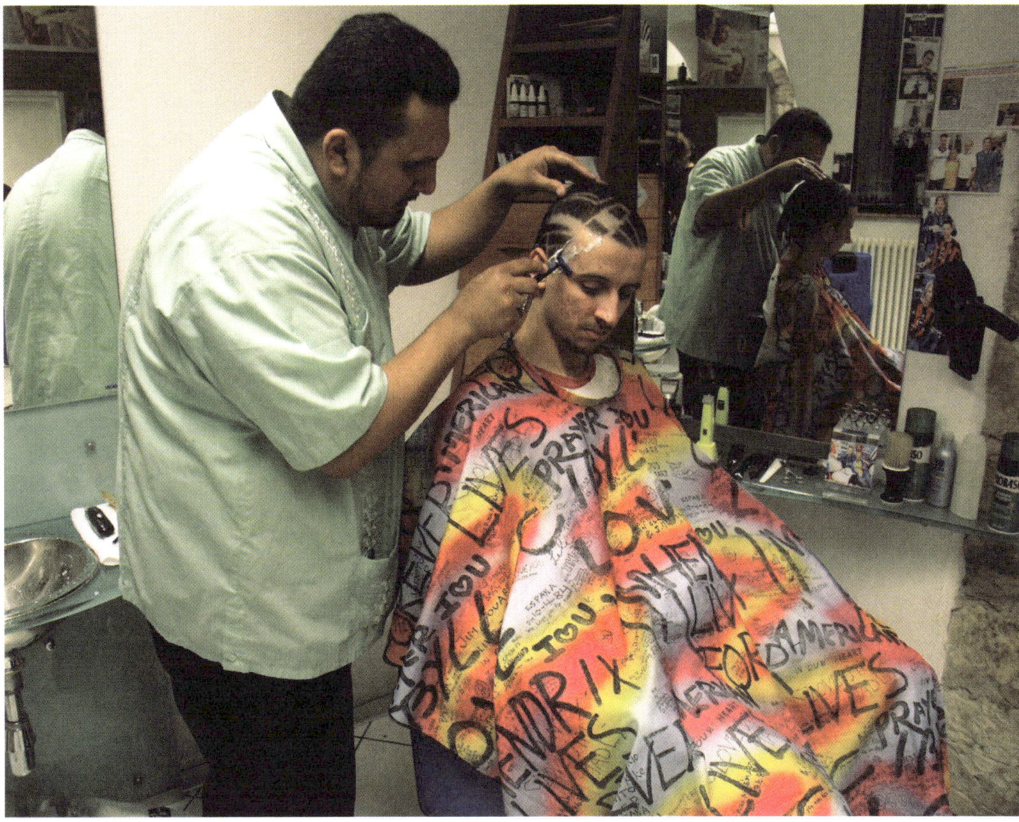

Haircut 2007
Performance
Salone Patton & Pedron, Trento, organised by Galleria Civica di Arte Contemporanea di Trento
Courtesy of the artist and Anna Helwing Gallery, Los Angeles

BIOGRAPHIES

PAWEL ALTHAMER
Born in 1967 in Warsaw, Poland, where he continues to live and work.

SELECTED EXHIBITIONS
Althamer's work has been included in numerous major exhibitions, including the Berlin Biennale (2006) and the Venice Biennale (2003). His solo exhibitions include those at the Pompidou Centre, Paris (2006) and Museum of Contemporary Art, Chicago (2003). Collections include Tate and Museum Ludwig, Cologne.

SELECTED BIBLIOGRAPHY

Ineke Kleijn (ed.), *Pawel Althamer: The Vincent van Gogh Bi-annual Award for Contemporary Art in Europe 2004*, exh. cat., Bonnefantenmuseum, Maastricht, Ostfildern Ruit 2004
Rita Kirsting, Grzegorz Kowalski and Joanna Mytkowska, *Arthur Zmijewski and Paweł Althamer*, exh. cat., Kunstverein für die Reinlande und Westfalen, Düsseldorf 2003
Paweł Althamer, *Bródno* 2000, exh. cat., Foksal Gallery Foundation, Warsaw 2000
Andrzej Przywara, *Pawel Althamer*, exh. cat., Kunsthalle Basel 1997

CEZARY BODZIANOWSKI
Born in 1968 in Łódz, Poland, where he continues to live and work.

SELECTED EXHIBITIONS
Solo exhibitions include those at Giti Nourbakhsch, Berlin (2006) and Cologne Kunstverein (2005).

SELECTED BIBLIOGRAPHY

I Love Paris, exh. cat., Foksal Gallery Foundation, Warsaw 2005
Cezary Bodzianowski, exh. cat., Foksal Gallery Foundation, Warsaw 2001

ULLA VON BRANDENBURG
Born in 1974 in Karlsruhe, Germany. She lives and works in Paris.

SELECTED EXHIBITIONS
Solo exhibitions include those at Art:Concept, Paris (2007); Produzentengalerie, Hamburg (2007); Palais de Tokyo, Paris (2006) and Kunsthalle Zürich (2006).

SELECTED BIBLIOGRAPHY

Anna-Catharina Gebbers, 'Ulla von Brandenburg', in *With no Trouble at All*, exh. cat., Kunstverein Glückstadt 2006
Jessica Morgan, 'Ulla von Brandenburg', *Artforum*, vol.44, no.10, Summer 2006
Robin Simpson, 'Charme Is a Trick of Visibility', in *Stipendium*, exh. cat., Kunstverein Hamburg 2006
Nora Sdun, 'Ulla von Brandenburg', in *Don't Accept Mañana*, exh. cat., Kunstverein Braunschweig 2006

JEREMY DELLER

Born in 1966 in London, where he continues to live and work.

SELECTED EXHIBITIONS

Solo exhibitions include those at Kunstverein Munich (2005), Barbican Art Gallery, London (2005) and BAWAG, Vienna (2005).

SELECTED BIBLIOGRAPHY

Jeremy Deller, Alan Kane and Bruce A. Haines, *Folk Archive: Contemporary Popular Art from the UK*, London 2005
Jeremy Deller, *After the Goldrush*, San Francisco 2002
Jeremy Deller, *The Uses of Literacy*, London 1999

TRISHA DONNELLY

Born in 1974 in San Francisco, where she continues to live and work.

SELECTED EXHIBITIONS

Solo exhibitions include those at Modern Art Oxford (2007), Kunsthalle Zürich (2005) and Cologne Kunstverein (2005).

SELECTED BIBLIOGRAPHY

Nancy Spector, 'Trisha Donnelly', in *Cream3*, London 2003
Trisha Donnelly, exh. cat., Air de Paris, Paris 2002
How Wonderful the World Exists, exh. cat., Casey Kaplan Gallery, New York 2002

GEOFFREY FARMER

Born in 1967 on Eagle Island, British Columbia. He currently lives and works in Vancouver, Canada.

SELECTED EXHIBITIONS

Solo exhibitions include those at Montreal Museum of Contemporary Art (2007) and Power Plant, Toronto (2005).

SELECTED BIBLIOGRAPHY

Jessica Morgan, 'First Take: Jessica Morgan on Geoffrey Farmer', *ArtForum*, vol.44, no.5, January 2006
Reid Shier, 'Buddies, Pals', in *Intertidal: Vancouver Art and Artists*, exh. cat., Muhka, Antwerp and Belkin Art Gallery, Vancouver 2005
Peter Culley and Reid Shier, *Geoffrey Farmer*, exh. cat., Contemporary Art Gallery, Vancouver 2003
Andrew Renton, 'Disappearing, Dislodging and Logging Off in B.C.', in Andrew Renton and Katherine Stout, *The Beachcombers*, The Drawing Room, London 2002
Renato Barilli, 'Art Drifts', in *Officina America*, exh. cat., Villa della Rose, Bologna 2002

ANDREA FRASER

Born in 1965 in Billings, Montana, U.S.A. She lives and works in New York and Los Angeles.

SELECTED EXHIBITIONS

Solo exhibitions include those at Friedrich Petzel Gallery, New York (2007), Hamburg Kunstverein (2003) and Belkin Art Gallery, Vancouver (2002).

SELECTED BIBLIOGRAPHY

Alexander Alberro (ed.), *Museum Highlights: The Writings of Andrea Fraser*, Cambridge 2005
'Andrea Fraser', *Kritisches Lexikon der Gegenwartskunst*, vol.69, no.5, 2005
New Video Work by Andrea Fraser, exh. cat., Belkin Art Gallery, Vancouver 2004
Andrea Fraser: Works 1984 to 2003, exh. cat., Kunstverein Hamburg 2003

DOMINIQUE GONZALEZ-FOERSTER

Born in 1965 in Strasbourg, France. She lives and works in Paris and Rio de Janeiro.

SELECTED EXHIBITIONS

Solo exhibitions include those at Musée d'Art Moderne de la Ville de Paris / ARC, Paris (2007); Kunsthalle Zürich (2004); Le Consortium, Dijon (2001) and Portikus, Frankfurt (2001).

SELECTED BIBLIOGRAPHY

Expodrome, exh. cat., Musée d'Art Moderne de la Ville de Paris / ARC, Paris 2007
Dominique Gonzalez-Foerster, *Tropicalisation!*, Antwerp and Zurich 2006
Dominique Gonzalez-Foerster, *Films*, exh. cat., Portikus, Frankfurt and Le Consortium, Dijon 2003
Stéphanie Moisdon-Trembley, *Dominique Gonzalez-Foerster*, Paris 2002
Dominique Gonzalez-Foerster: 88:88 – Moment, exh. cat., Kaiser Wilhelm Museum, Krefeld 1998

JEPPE HEIN

Born in 1974 in Copenhagen, Denmark. He currently lives and works in Berlin.

SELECTED EXHIBITIONS

Solo exhibitions include those at Barbican Art Gallery, London (2007), Pompidou Centre, Paris (2005) and The Moore Space, Miami (2005).

SELECTED BIBLIOGRAPHY

Jeppe Hein (ed.), *Jeppe Hein Until Now*, London 2006
Jeppe Hein, exh. cat., Centre Pompidou, Paris 2005
Finn Janning (ed.), 'The Vital Coincidence' in *Jeppe Hein*, Cologne 2003

RENATA LUCAS

Born in 1971 in Ribeirão Preto, Brazil. She lives and works in Rio de Janeiro.

SELECTED EXHIBITIONS

Solo exhibitions include those at Redcat, Los Angeles (2007); Milan Antonio, São Paulo (2006) and Gentil Carioca, Rio de Janeiro (2005).

SELECTED BIBLIOGRAPHY

Lisette Sagnado, 'Renata Lucas', *Frieze*, no.107, May 2007
Lorenzo Mammi, *Renata Lucas*, exh. cat., Prémio SESI-CNI, Marcantonio Vilaça, Museo National de Bellas Artes, Rio de Janeiro 2005
Rodrigo Moura, 'Beyond Sculpture', *Flash Art*, no.230, June 2003
Tatiana Blass, 'O espaço e sua réplica', in *Comum de dois*, exh. cat., Centro Universitário Maria Antonia, São Paulo 2001

RITA MCBRIDE

Born in 1960 in Des Moines, Iowa. She lives and works in Düsseldorf.

SELECTED EXHIBITIONS

Solo exhibitions include those at Alexander and Bonin, New York (2006), P.S.1 Sculpture Centre, Long Island (2004) and Witte de With, Rotterdam (1997).

SELECTED BIBLIOGRAPHY

Rita McBride and Glen Rubsamen (eds.) *Futureways*, Vancouver and New York 2004
Rita McBride and Erin Cosgrove (eds.), *Heartways: The Exploits of Genny O*, Vancouver and New York 2004
Margrit Brehm, David Gray, Bartomeu Marí, Jessica Morgan, Dirk Snauwaert and Matthias Winzen (eds.) *Werskshow*, exh. cat., Staaliche Kunsthalle, Baden-Baden 2000
Bartomeu Marí, Christian Rattemeyer, Paloma Schultz and Dominic van der Boogerd, *Arena*, exh. cat., Witte de With, Rotterdam 1998

ROMAN ONDÁK

Born in 1966 in Slovakia. He lives and works in Bratislava, Slovakia and Berlin, Germany.

SELECTED EXHIBITIONS

Solo exhibitions include those at BAK, Utrecht (2007); Tate Modern, London (2006); CAC Brétigny, France (2006) and Cologne Kunstverein (2004).

SELECTED BIBLIOGRAPHY

Frank Frangenberg, Hans Ulrich Obrist, Georg Schöllhammer and Igor Zabel, *Roman Ondák*, exh. cat., Cologne Kunstverein 2005
Jan Verwoert, 'Taking a Line for a Walk', *Frieze*, no.90, 2005
Jessica Morgan, 'First Take', *Artforum*, January 2005
Igor Zabel, 'Roman Ondák', in *Cream3*, London 2003

MARKUS SCHINWALD

Born in 1973 in Salzburg, Austria. He lives and works in Vienna.

SELECTED EXHIBITIONS

Solo exhibitions include those at Sprengl Museum, Hanover (2004); Kunstverein Frankfurt (2004); TAV Gallery, Taipei (2003); Kunstverein Goldegg (2002); Moderna Museet, Stockholm (2001) and MAK Center for Art and Architecture, Los Angeles (2000).

SELECTED BIBLIOGRAPHY

Markus Heinzelmann and Nicolaus Schafhausen (eds.), *Markus Schinwald*, New York 2004
Markus Schinwald: Tableau Twain, exh. cat., Kunstverein Frankfurt 2004
Markus Schinwald, exh. cat., Moderna Museet, Stockholm 2002

TINO SEHGAL

Born in 1976 in London. He lives and works in Berlin.

SELECTED EXHIBITIONS

Solo exhibitions include those at Fundação Serralves, Porto (2005); Van Abbemuseum, Eindhoven (2004) and Musée des Beaux-Arts, Nantes (2004). A series of three solo exhibitions over a three-year period was staged at the Institute of Contemporary Arts, London (2004–7).

SELECTED BIBLIOGRAPHY

Stephen Hoban (ed.), *Hugo Boss Prize 2006: Guggenheim Museum*, exh. cat., Solomon R. Guggenheim Museum, New York 2006
Catherine Wood, 'Tino Sehgal', in Beatrix Ruf and Clarrie Wallis (eds.), *Tate Triennial 2006: New British Art*, exh. cat., Tate Britain, London 2006
I Promise it's Political, exh. cat., Museum Ludwig, Cologne 2002
A Little Bit of History Repeated, exh. cat., Kunst-Werke, Berlin 2001

CATHERINE SULLIVAN

Born in 1968 in Los Angeles, U.S.A. She lives and works in Chicago.

SELECTED EXHIBITIONS

Solo exhibitions include those at Tate Modern, London (2005–6), Zurich Kunsthalle (2005), Vienna Secession (2005) and Renaissance Society at the University of Chicago (2002). In addition, her theatrical work has been staged at independent venues in Los Angeles, Chicago, Tokyo and Lyon.

SELECTED BIBLIOGRAPHY

Catherine Sullivan, *Film and Theater Works – 2002–2004*, Dijon 2006
Pierre-Yves Fonfon, Sean Griffin, Zoltán Krapschutt, Wolf-Dieter Schlünz and Catherine Sullivan, *Catherine Sullivan, The Chittendens, Discrete Manifestation with Music by Sean Griffin*, exh. cat., Vienna Secession and Tate Modern, London 2005

Catherine Wood, 'An Actor Prepares', *Frieze*, no.95, November–December 2005
Hamza Walker and Russell Ferguson, *Catherine Sullivan: Five Economies (big hunt/little hunt)*, exh. cat., UCLA Hammer Museum, Los Angeles and Renaissance Society at the University of Chicago 2002

MARIO YBARRA JR.

Born in 1973 in Los Angeles, where he continues to live and work.

SELECTED EXHIBITIONS

Solo exhibitions include those at Anna Helwig Gallery, Los Angeles (2007) and Art Positions, Art Basel Miami Beach (2006). He has also been included in group exhibitions at the Institute of Contemporary Arts, London and the Serpentine Gallery, London (both 2006).

SELECTED BIBLIOGRAPHY

Gilane Tawadros, John Gill and Jens Hoffmann (eds.) *Alien Nation*, exh. cat., Institute of Contemporary Arts, London 2007
Andrew Berardini, 'Mario Ybarra Jr. Bring me the head of ...' *Art Review*, February 2007
Jens Hoffmann, 'First Take: Mario Ybarra Jr.', *Artforum*, January 2007

NOTES

ART MEETS THEATRE: THE MIDDLE ZONE

[1] Frank Stella, 'New Nihilism or New Art?', Interview with Bruce Glaser, 1964; reprinted in James Meyer, *Modernism,* London and New York 2000, p.199.

[2] Michael Fried, 'Art & Objecthood' (1967), in *Art & Objecthood: Essays and Reviews*, Chicago 1998, p.155.

[3] In 1930, Bertolt Brecht argued against the theatre's conventional dramatic style. This must, he said, be 'given up', intended, as it was, 'to produce hypnosis … to induce sordid intoxication'. In a chart contrasting the qualities of this kind of theatricality with his own 'Epic' style, Brecht proposed that 'argument' should replace 'suggestion', 'reason' replace 'feeling' and that rather than being immersed 'in the thick of it', the spectator should stand 'outside' to 'study' the play. Bertolt Brecht, 'The Modern Theatre is the Epic Theatre', in *Brecht on Theatre: The Development of an Aesthetic*, trans. John Willett, London 2001, pp.37–8.

[4] Benjamin Buchloh, 'Memory Lessons and Historic Tableaux: James Coleman's Archaeology of Spectacle', in *Neo Avant-Garde and Culture Industry*, Cambridge, Massachusetts 2004, pp.141–78.

[5] Max Herrmann, Lecture on 27 June 1920, cited by Erika Fischer-Lichte in *Theatre, Sacrificec, Ritual – Exploring Forms of Political Theatre*), London 2005.

[6] Peter Brook, *The Empty Space* (1968), Harmondsworth 1972, p.11.

[7] Ibid., p.11.

[8] This observation is very much related to the self-consciously performative approach to remaking work in past historical styles: Constructivist or Bauhaus in the work of Lucy McKenzie and Paulina Olowska, for example.

[9] Jeremy Deller, Interview with John Slyce, *Flash Art*, January–February 2003, p.76.

[10] Selim O. Khan-Megadomov, *Rodchenko: The Complete Work*, London 1986, p.202.

[11] In this sense, Michael Fried had a valid point: his anxiety about the staging of his own presence was no doubt literally underwritten by his awareness of these performances in which a role for the person was clearly defined and choreographed in relation to the object.

[12] Melanie Gilligan, 'The Beggar's Pantomime', *Artforum*, Summer 2007, pp.426–33.

[13] David Graeber, 'Fetishism as Social Creativity, or Fetishes Are Gods in the Process of Construction', in *Anthropological Theory*, vol.5, 2005, p.416.

[14] Ibid., p.425.

[15] Ibid., p.426.
[16] Ibid., p.432.
[17] Brecht 2001, pp.37–8.
[18] Fried 1967, p.164.
[19] Graeber 2005, p.432.
[20] David Graeber, 'The False Coin of our own Dreams', in *Towards an Anthropological Theory of Value*, New York 2001, p.230.
[21] Jacques Rancière, 'The Emancipated Spectator', reprinted in *Artrforum*, March 2007.
[22] Tadeusz Kantor, 'Teatr Wydarzen (The Happening Theatre)', in *Tadeusz Kantor: Metamorfozy, Teksy o latach 1838–1974*, ed. K. Plesniarowicz, p.416, cited in Jaroslaw Suchan, 'Kantor's Real Illusion and Other True Fictions', *The Impossible Theatre,* exh. cat., Kunsthalle Vienna 2006, p.18.

JEREMY DELLER

[1] Tom Lubbock, 'When History Repeats Itself Too Soon', *Independent*, 19 June 2001.
[2] *Off Limits: 40 Artangel Projects*, London 2002, p.91.
[3] Ibid.
[4] Ibid.

ANDREA FRASER

[1] Notes by Andrea Fraser in *Andrea Fraser Works: 1984 to 2003*, Hamburg and Cologne 2003, p.218.
[2] See note 4, *Performance Script for Museum Highlights: A Gallery Talk* (1989), in *Andrea Fraser: Works 1984 to 2003*, exh. cat., Kunstverein Hamburg and Cologne 2003, p.251.
[3] Yilmaz Dziewior, 'Interview with Andrea Fraser', in *Andrea Fraser Works: 1984 to 2003*, p.99.
[4] Ibid.

DOMINIQUE GONZALEZ-FOERSTER

[1] Dominique Gonzalez-Foerster in *Dominique Gonzalez-Foerster: 88:88 – Moment*, exh. cat., Kaiser Wilhem Museum, Krefeld 1998.
[2] *Promenade* 2007, in collaboration with Christophe Van Huffel, installation shown in Expodrome, ARC – Musée d'Art Moderne de la Ville de Paris in 2007.

JEPPE HEIN

[1] Barbara Steiner, 'Double Bind', in Jeppe Hein (ed.), *Jeppe Hein until Now*, London 2006, p.78.

TINO SEGHAL

[1] Tim Etchells, 'The Show Must Go On', *Dance Theatre Journal*, June 2004.
[2] *Instead of allowing some thing to rise up to your face dancing bruce and dan and other things* 2000.
[3] *This is progaganda* 2002.

4 *This is good* 2001; *This is new* 2003 and *This exhibition* 2004.
5 *This is right* 2003; *This Success or this Failure* 2007.
6 *This objective of that object* 2004.
7 *This Progress*, Institute of Contemporary Arts, London 2006.

CATHERINE SULLIVAN
1 Catherine Sullivan interviewed by Russell Ferguson, in *Catherine Sullivan: Five Economies (big hunt/little hunt)*, ex.cat., by UCLA Hammer Museum, Los Angeles and Renaissance Society at the University of Chicago 2002.
2 *Catherine Sullivan: The Chittendens: Discrete Manifestations with Music by Sean Griffin*, exh. cat., Vienna Succession and Tate Modern, London 2005

PHOTO CREDITS

Photographers
pp.29, 41 Tate Photography
p.33 Monika Chojnicka
p.39 Martin Jenkinson
pp.44–5 Rafael Goldchain
pp.51–2 Anders Berg
p.53 Holger Hübsch / Jeppe Hein
p.57 Hermann Selhaus
p.59 Wolfgang Woessner
pp.61–2 Marcus Schinwald
pp.66–7 David Moquay
p.71 Hugo Muñoz